A VERY SHORT,
FAIRLY INTERESTING AND
REASONABLY CHEAP BOOK ABOUT
MANAGEMENT RESEARCH

Praise for *A Very Short, Fairly Interesting and Reasonably Cheap Book About Management Research*

'By providing a lively and accessible introduction to management research – which is theoretically informed and methodologically inclusive – Bell and Thorpe's timely text offers illuminating responses to a wide range of issues raised by students entering this field.'

Hugh Willmott, Professor of Organization Studies, Cardiff Business School, UK

'Among the weighty tomes on management research methods, this lively, elegant and readable guide is welcome indeed. Emma and Richard carry their deep knowledge of the field lightly, distilling complex debates and terminology into a lucid navigation of the key issues in management research. It should be on every graduate student's bookshelf – and probably on their supervisor's as well.'

Amanda Sinclair, Professorial Fellow, Melbourne Business School, University of Melbourne, Australia

Also in this series

Jim Blythe, *A Very Short, Fairly Interesting and Reasonably Cheap Book about* **Studying Marketing**

Ann L Cunliffe, *A Very Short, Fairly Interesting and Reasonably Cheap Book about* **Management**

Chris Carter, Stewart R Clegg and Martin Kornberger, *A Very Short, Fairly Interesting and Reasonably Cheap Book About* **Studying Strategy**

George Cairns and Martyna Sliwa, *A Very Short, Fairly Interesting and Reasonably Cheap Book about* **International Business**

Brad Jackson and Ken Parry, *A Very Short Fairly Interesting and Reasonably Cheap Book About* **Studying Leadership**, 2nd Edition

Bob Garvey, *A Very Short, Fairly Interesting and Reasonably Cheap Book About* **Coaching and Mentoring**

Chris Grey, *A Very Short, Fairly Interesting and Reasonably Cheap Book About* **Studying Organizations**, 3rd Edition

David Silverman, *A Very Short, Fairly Interesting and Reasonably Cheap Book about* **Qualitative Research**, 2nd Edition

A VERY SHORT, FAIRLY INTERESTING AND REASONABLY CHEAP BOOK ABOUT MANAGEMENT RESEARCH

EMMA BELL AND RICHARD THORPE

Los Angeles | London | New Delhi
Singapore | Washington DC

Los Angeles | London | New Delhi
Singapore | Washington DC

SAGE Publications Ltd
1 Oliver's Yard
55 City Road
London EC1Y 1SP

SAGE Publications Inc.
2455 Teller Road
Thousand Oaks, California 91320

SAGE Publications India Pvt Ltd
B 1/I 1 Mohan Cooperative Industrial Area
Mathura Road
New Delhi 110 044

SAGE Publications Asia-Pacific Pte Ltd
3 Church Street
#10-04 Samsung Hub
Singapore 049483

© Emma Bell and Richard Thorpe 2013

First published 2013

Editor: Kirsty Smy
Editorial assistant: Nina Smith
Production editor: Sarah Cooke
Copyeditor: Christine Bitten
Proofreader: Lynda Watson
Indexer: Martin Hargreaves
Marketing manager: Alison Borg
Cover design: Wendy Scott
Typeset by: C&M Digitals (P) Ltd, Chennai, India
Printed and bound by CPI Group (UK) Ltd,
Croydon, CR04YY

Library of Congress Control Number: 2013933371

British Library Cataloguing in Publication data

A catalogue record for this book is available from
the British Library

MIX
Paper from
responsible sources
FSC
www.fsc.org   FSC® C013604

ISBN 978-1-44620-161-9
ISBN 978-1-44620-162-6 (pbk)

Contents

About the Authors

Emma Bell is Professor of Management and Organisation Studies and Head of the Centre for Economics and Management at Keele Management School.

Her research is framed by a desire to understand cultures and belief systems in organizations. She has also studied business improvement initiatives and organizational change. Emma was a member of the British Academy of Management Council, and is current co-chair of the US Academy of Management Critical Management Studies Division.

Her early working life included a period as a graduate trainee in the UK National Health Service. Emma's PhD was an ethnographic study of payment systems and organizational time in the chemical industry. She has always been interested in methods and methodologies of management research, and the ways in which management knowledge is created.

Recently, Emma has been involved in a number of projects related to visual analysis of organizations and management. She is a founding member of InVisio – the International Network of Visual Studies in Organizations, and worked on an ESRC Researcher Development Initiative to promote the development of visual analysis in management research.

Richard Thorpe is Professor of Management Development and Pro-Dean for Research at Leeds University Business School.

His research interests have included: performance, entrepreneurship, knowledge and leadership, as well as research methods in management research. His early career as a management trainee on a Clarks programme informed the way his ethos has developed.

Following a period in industry his first academic appointment was as a researcher at Strathclyde University in the Pay and Reward Research Centre. There, as a consequence of the research conducted he developed close links with practitioners, intermediaries and policy makers, something he has strived to maintain as his career progressed. Common themes in his work are: a strong commitment to conducting research in collaboration with practitioners; a focus on action and change; an interest in – and commitment to – the development of doctoral students; and the development of capacity within the sector.

Richard has been past president and chair of the British Academy of Management and a member of the ESRC Training and Development Board. He is currently chair of the Society for the Advancement of Management Studies.

Acknowledgements

The ideas in this book have been developed over a long time, through conversations with a great many colleagues and students.

From Leeds, a number of PhD students have been helpful in enabling us to identify the issues and concerns that they face as early career academics. These include Gerard Duff, Charlotte Coleman, Paul Ellwood and Lena Kruckenberg. In particular we would like to thank Lena Kruckenberg and Charlotte Coleman for their help and insights at various stages of the writing process.

Emma would like to acknowledge the Doctoral Society at University of Edinburgh Business School; faculty and doctoral students at University of Glasgow Business School; faculty of the University of Business and Technology in Jeddah, Saudi Arabia; faculty and doctoral students at Sobey School of Business, St Mary's University Canada; PhD students and colleagues at the Open University Business School; Sunita Singh Sengupta at the Faculty of Management Studies, University of Delhi, India; and members of the British Academy of Management Research Methods Special Interest Group. She would like to thank Haneen Shoaib for helping to restore her faith in the PhD supervision process. Finally she would also like to thank Scott Taylor, her partner and companion in conferences, fieldwork and writing.

Several people very generously commented on parts of the book at various stages. These included Sadhvi Dar at Queen Mary University of London, Hugh Willmott at Cardiff University, Amanda Sinclair at Melbourne University, Bill Lee at Sheffield University, Kate Kenny at National University of Ireland, Chris Grey at Royal Holloway University of London, Ann Cunliffe at University of Leeds, Joep Cornelissen at VU University of Amsterdam and Dvora Yanow at Wageningen University in the Netherlands. Thanks also to Albert Mills for permission to write about Sobey School of Business at Saint Mary's University in Canada. Their insights and encouragement were invaluable.

Finally we would like to thank our editors at Sage for their help and encouragement throughout this process and also for permission for use of the section on disciplined imagination, a version of which appeared in the third edition of *Management Research* (2008) by Easterby-Smith et al (London: Sage).

Should You Buy This Book?

This book is mainly intended for university students doing a dissertation based on original research in the field of management. This includes students studying for a Bachelors or Masters Degree in management, as well as MBA, DBA and PhD students. It is also written with academics in mind who do research in the field of management.

You should buy this book if:

- you are a curious person who is always asking how and why management is the way it is;
- you are currently studying for a university level qualification in management and you have to do a dissertation based on original research;
- you want to know how and why people do management research;
- you sat through an entire research methods course but you can't remember much about it;
- you are wondering why you decided to become a management researcher, and sometimes feeling doubts about it;
- you are finding the process of doing management research isolating and you would like to do something about this.

You shouldn't buy this book if:

- you don't ask questions and you aren't curious about management;
- you just want to memorise what the textbooks say and recite it;
- you want an instructional guide to using data analysis software;
- you think that research enables managerial problems to be solved once and for all.

If you do buy this book and want to talk to us about it, you can email one or both of us at: e.bell@keele.ac.uk and r.thorpe@lubs.leeds.ac.uk

Introduction

Why Management Research Matters to Us

> You do not have to believe anything about theory and methodology that is told you pretentiously and sanctimoniously by other sociologists – including myself.
>
> (George Caspar Homans, 1964: 975)

This short book is based on the assertion that management research can be an extremely interesting and potentially worthwhile activity. While it doesn't result in a cure for cancer, or the discovery of alternative energy sources, the influence of management on all aspects of our lives is enormous. Attempts to understand management, through detailed investigation and critical analysis, must therefore be worthwhile. This book is about how management research is done, including the underlying assumptions and methods of inquiry that guide it. In other words, it is about *how* management research happens, rather than *what* it produces. This is important because ideas about management are significantly shaped by the philosophies, methodologies and methods used to produce them.

Your reasons for reading this book may be because you are a student doing a degree in management contemplating your dissertation or research project and wondering where on earth to start. For you, management research may be a part-time and temporary activity. The book is also written for those seeking to become a management researcher in a more permanent sense, by enrolling on a PhD or a DBA programme. By management research we mean studies relating to any aspect of management, work and organisation. This includes the various sub-fields of employee relations, human resource management, organisation studies, marketing, strategy, tourism, as well as accounting, economics and finance.

Most people understand management research to be an area of study that draws on a broad range of social scientific disciplines including sociology, psychology, economics and anthropology. Many would consider management research to be a field of inquiry, rather than an academic discipline in its own right, because the conventions that determine how research is done are inseparable from these longer established disciplines. This is why management research is often referred to as an interdisciplinary field which blends together ideas and methods from other disciplines and applies them to the subject of management. Having said this, a great deal of management research is not really very interdisciplinary at all, as many management researchers favour just one discipline like economics or psychology, which they rely heavily on in their research.

This book has also been written with the purpose of encouraging everyone connected with management research – including ourselves – to take a long hard look at what we do, and why we do it. In all fields of practice, including management, this can be an important and constructive thing to do from time to time. So rather than telling you how we do management research and explaining how you can acquire the skills, knowledge and self identity to enable you to be like us, we want to talk about the process of management research and leave you to decide how to engage with it. We do not mean to suggest that it is just up to new researchers to deal with what is problematic about management research. But new researchers can play an important role in questioning certain forms of practice by looking upon these issues with fresh eyes.

Management research is an area where a great deal of the skills, knowledge and competence that goes into doing it, is acquired tacitly, rather than explicitly. Some researchers might say this is because it is something that can only be learned through practice, supported by the expert advice of your supervisor. While there is a lot that can be learned by doing management research, we are somewhat suspicious of the mystique that surrounds such an approach and the dependency and isolation it can create for the person doing the learning. We hope that this book will go some way towards dispelling the idea that management research is something that can only be learned by doing what your supervisor tells you to do.

This book then, is based on our own and colleagues' experiences of management research. Along the way, we explore the issues that we have found challenging, including how research happens, and how it comes to be written up in published form. As most management researchers are only too ready to acknowledge in private, published versions of research are prone to a reconstructed logic that doesn't always demonstrate either how the research was conceived, or how it was carried out. Research is a messy, serendipitous and unpredictable process. Hatch (1996) recommends that researchers don't reveal this messy reality until they are well established as a career academic, because it is dangerous to do so before then. Our aim here is to offer an insight into what Goffman (1959) would call the 'backstage' of management research: a place that is obscured from the glare of the front-stage floodlights, where the management researcher is required to give a convincing public performance to external audiences.

Van Maanen (1988) refers to this as telling 'tales of the field'. In doing this our hope is to capture some of the excitement involved in doing management research as well as to clarify some of the dilemmas that researchers frequently face.

A different kind of book

It is important to say that this is not a textbook. It does not explain how to do management research. It does not set out all the various methods and techniques that can be used in management research, nor does it give you a template for designing and carrying out a research project of your own. Grey (2009), in the original book that launched this series, is rather scathing about big heavy, expensive textbooks that provide exhaustive, and possibly exhausting, coverage of a subject, often with copious illustrations, diagrams and bullet points. To an extent, we are inclined to agree with him. But we have each been involved in writing textbooks. Emma has written *Business Research Methods* with Alan Bryman, published by Oxford University Press and now in its third edition. Richard has written *Management Research*, with Mark Easterby Smith and Paul Jackson, first published by Sage in 1991, now in its fourth edition. Each of these books is quite successful and students sometimes tell us that they find them helpful. It would be hypocritical of us to disparage such books as pointless and counterproductive, and to be perfectly honest we don't believe that they are, in part because they are read by people who claim that they help them to do management research, which is something we feel passionately about.

But we do think there is something missing from management research methods textbooks, even those we have written. The advice that management research methods textbooks provide is not dissimilar in style to the recipe books of the well-known English cook and writer, Delia Smith, whose reputation is founded on providing clear instruction and reassuring advice in a way which has got a lot of people interested in cooking who might otherwise not have been confident enough to experiment with new ingredients and recipes. 'Doing a Delia' even has an entry in some dictionaries. The problem with this approach to research, and possibly also to cooking, is that it doesn't necessarily give you the confidence and understanding to enable you to improvise, for example if you can't obtain the recipe ingredient exactly specified.

To understand how such a situation arises, you need to understand the nature of textbooks, and why readers are encouraged to turn to them. As Grey (2009) argues in relation to the study of organisations, textbooks are a bit like the Bible, providing an orthodox view on a subject. They tend to be positioned – by publishers, authors and even readers – as authoritative sources of knowledge. Buying them, consulting them, or even just carrying them with you on the bus, can bring a certain comfort or reassurance from the thought that they contain a degree of certainty and truth. The trouble is that management research has a habit of unfolding in ways that are messy and unpredictable, primarily because it involves the study of organisations and people. But you wouldn't necessarily realise this from reading methods textbooks.

There are several reasons for this which we will discuss later, but for the moment it is enough to say that it is not always in researchers' interests to reveal the process of management research as anything other than logical, rational and predictable, which is why we feel there is a need for a different kind of book.

Can this be an interesting book?

A further issue to note by way of introduction is that the title of this book promises, among other things, that the content will be interesting. This could be seen as a particular challenge in relation to management research because quite a few people have recently said it is not very interesting. For example, Bartunek et al. (2006) say that although the prestigious management research journals have a widely respected reputation for publishing very competent research, not many of the articles published are considered interesting, in terms of engaging readers' attention or challenging commonly held assumptions about a subject. The vast majority of the articles published in this type of journal rely on quantitative techniques of data collection, such as large-scale surveys, and involve statistical methods of interpretation. But those that readers found most interesting were the ones that used qualitative research methods, such as unstructured interviews and participant observation. Some would say this is because qualitative researchers have 'already departed from mainstream methods, [and] have less to lose by studying odd topics and taking theoretical risks' (Barley, 2006: 19).

There are other reasons why management research is not often seen as very interesting. You may have heard of a game played in management meetings called buzzword bingo. Instead of having random numbers on your bingo card, you have management buzzwords like 'think outside the box', 'going forward', 'pushing the envelope', 'world-class' and 'helicopter view'. The aim of the game is to see how many of the words are mentioned in the meeting and the person who wins is the one who checks off all the words on their card first. But rather than shout BINGO (which would reveal to your colleagues in the meeting who weren't playing the game that you were not taking their pearls of managerial wisdom entirely seriously), you devise a secret code to communicate with your fellow players, such as coughing surreptitiously. A similar game could be devised for management research. A brief skim through recent issues of the journal *Academy of Management Review* reveals remarkable similarity in the terminology used in papers. Here are a few examples:

- We present an alternative to previous conceptual models through the work of [x].
- We combine insights from this field and that field.
- Drawing on theories of [y] we develop the [z] model.
- I adopt a [t] perspective to examine....
- Through this review, we develop a series of theoretical precepts to guide future development of the field.

Next time you read a management research article see how many similar phrases you can find. Not only does this highly codified and abstract language make articles difficult to understand, it also makes them terminally dull. Through formulaic repetition, the words are rendered 'dead on the page', and that doesn't really make you want to read them. Perrow describes this as a process of covering articles with elite journal 'asphalt', as a result of which any trace of 'gentle irony, humour, evocative phrasing, even active verb construction, let alone any unscientific hesitancy' (Perrow, 1995: 213) is removed. Part of the reason for this may be because management researchers have become frightened to be blunt because they fear being perceived as crude in their way of thinking. Hence the whole practice of presenting management research becomes couched in complex jargon and terminology that systematises and standardises the whole affair and protects the researcher from potential criticism. As a result, management researchers and practitioners end up speaking different languages and much of the knowledge that is created doesn't get disseminated very effectively. This has led some people to argue that we need to develop different ways of writing about management research, to avoid the pompous, impenetrable writing that seems to be driven by a desire to accrue papers as ends in themselves, rather than as a way of communicating with others (Grey and Sinclair, 2006). They lament the stilted and distant nature of research writing, which results in very few management practitioners actually reading what is published in scholarly books and journals

(Dane, 2011). Yet despite these arguments, if anything the esoteric nature of much management research writing appears only to be increasing.

So if management research is widely viewed as rather dull, how can we possibly hope to write a book on this subject that is interesting? Added to this, we know from talking to management researchers and educators at other universities who teach research methods that students tend to find such courses somewhat boring (not because of the teaching we might add), but because they find it difficult to relate technical ideas about research methods to the actual process of doing research. It's often only after *doing* their research that any of it makes sense.

It is also important to understand the rules according to which knowledge is constructed through research, even if you don't plan to carry out any research yourself. A good deal of what is talked about in this book relates to how judgements of quality and value are made in relation to management research. If you are reading this book you are probably a consumer of management research, studying the subject at university where what you are taught is based on published research which eventually gets distilled down into textbooks and onto Power-Point slides, and delivered to students in the classroom. Being able to ask questions about the knowledge claims presented to you is incredibly important, especially in the digital age, when virtually anyone can publish anything on the internet.

So you need to be a well informed consumer of management knowledge. This relies on understanding how knowledge is produced and whether or not it can be relied upon as a basis from which to make decisions and take action. To understand what the alternative looks like, take a look at the numerous websites where a whole gamut of management research is presented, including the ever-popular Maslow's Hierarchy of Needs. Here you will find virtually no critical analysis of this research, even though much current research disputes the usefulness of Maslow's theory and the methodology upon which it is based, and also highlights its cultural specificity.

We cannot simply blame the internet for these problems. For management education relies on certain widely taught theories that remain popular despite a substantial volume of respected research that challenges them (Watson, 1996). So rather than being spoon fed a small proportion of management research selected by your lecturer or tutor, we want you to be an active user of management knowledge who can trace back to the original source and evaluate it. Having an understanding of the process through which data is collected, analysed and interpreted is fundamental to this.

How we became management researchers

Let's start by telling you how we became management researchers. Richard started out as a management trainee at the Clarks shoe factory doing what was then known as work study. This involved measuring the time and sequence of work tasks on the shop floor so managers could organise them more efficiently. At this point he was focused on finding solutions to managerial problems. But as he became more experienced in management research, he became increasingly conscious of the immense difficulties involved in developing generalisable propositions about management, due in part to the vast cultural and historical differences in its practice. Richard is now approaching the end of his career as a management researcher, and moving ever further away from the idea that there is a stable body of management knowledge that applies across contexts, and even more towards the view that management knowledge is highly situationally specific.

Emma started her career as a management trainee in the UK National Health Service in the early 1990s. Her first job involved being responsible for the implementation of the government-sponsored people management initiative *Investors in People*. At first she couldn't understand why the medical professionals in the various hospital departments where she was working were so hostile towards the initiative. After leaving her job in the NHS to start a PhD in management, she carried out a project together with colleagues to explore managerial and employee perceptions surrounding the initiative. For Emma, this research was not primarily about doing research to solve a managerial problem, but trying to make sense of her own managerial experience, and through this to try to understand organisations a little better.

Although these stories highlight what management research often fails to do, in the sense of finding solutions to problems that transcend boundaries of time and place, they also draw attention to what management research *does do*, by enabling you as a researcher to step back from your situated experience of management and analyse it within a broader cultural and historical context. What is more, through disseminating the findings from management research to practising managers, students and other management researchers, it is possible for others to gain insight from them. In short, we don't agree with the idea that the purpose of research is to study management scientifically, and that this results in the production of a body of absolute knowledge which enables human progress through rational application. But we do think the purpose of management research is to generate situated understandings of complex phenomena which form the basis for more informed and reflective managerial practice.

Schon's (1983) concept of the reflective practitioner offers a useful way of thinking about this. Schon argues that professions like management lack a body of secure knowledge to guide practice, and that managers often deal with ideas that are ill-structured and face problems with no clear solutions. This has considerable implications for management research, for if there is no possibility of building any kind of theory other than a 'theory of action', which is intuitive and must be based on practical experience, what then is the purpose of management research? Does it lead to more effective managers, happier employees, greater organisational effectiveness, better products and services? Or does it enable us to understand the pervasive influence of management on almost every aspect of our lives?

One thing that will become clear as you read this book is that there is considerable ambiguity surrounding the answer to this question and different groups of management researchers answer it in quite different ways. Some researchers emphasise a technical understanding of management, as a process akin to engineering, others emphasise its political nature. Some see management research as having an inherently positive effect on society; others remain suspicious and antagonistic about its influence. Some researchers study management as a rational, cognitive process, whereas others see management as a much broader phenomenon affected by political, cultural and historical influences.

What you will find in this book

It is usual at this stage in an introduction to provide a summary of how the text is structured. In the first chapter we embark on a search for management research by considering what distinguishes it from other analytical activities related to management, like consultancy and journalism. We also introduce the idea that management research is a community and discuss the process whereby management researchers learn their craft and communicate it to others. Chapter 2 examines the purpose of management research by exploring two, sometimes conflicting, demands that affect management research: relevance and legitimacy. In Chapter 3 we delve deeper into management research by exploring the various philosophical traditions that researchers follow in their pursuit of knowledge. This chapter uses an extended religious metaphor to chart the various churches, small gods, high priests and disciples associated with each. Although this is not how philosophies of management knowledge are conventionally presented, we hope to convince you of the richness of this metaphor.

In the next three chapters we focus on issues relating to the practice of management research that affect how you engage with it. Chapter 4 begins by reviewing the paradigm wars which have been waged around management research and how attitudes towards quantitative and qualitative research have been reconfigured, partly as a result of the growth in mixed methods research. In Chapter 5 we explore the process of theorising in management research, which is an often overlooked aspect of the research process. Chapter 6 involves stepping back from the research act to reflect on the ethics and identity work involved in being a management researcher. In the Conclusion, attention turns towards encouraging you to think about the kind of management researcher you want to be, in the light of the ideas presented. As the book is short, arguments are made briefly and complex issues presented simply. But there are many other detailed books and articles about management research that you can read, as indicated by the reference list.

As you read you will notice that management research is characterised by a substantial amount of fairly complex and esoteric terminology, including numerous 'ologies' and 'isms' that are used to label various approaches and differentiate them from each other. This can be rather daunting and off-putting, especially initially, when it seems that the people using the terminology are speaking an entirely different language, one which you fear you will never be fluent in. Yet these ideas are crucial in uncovering the assumptions that inform the practice of management research.

As with learning any language, it is a matter of familiarity. We have approached the writing of this book in a way which encourages immersion, rather than systematic learning. This is rather like finding yourself in a country where they speak a different language and you have to learn a few words in order to buy something to eat and drink, instead of studying lots of books about grammar and memorising lists of vocabulary before you get there. You will therefore find that the terminology is explained as the arguments are presented, rather than set out in advance. If this terminology is new to you, it might seem a little odd, but familiarising yourself with these words can help you to learn the language for yourself.

As a general principle, it is important for management researchers to consider why they do research and the purposes it serves, which is what we try to do in this book. What follows is intended to be polemical as well as informative. This is because we are worried that some things have gone wrong in management research and we want to consider what these problems are. You might be thinking 'so why don't you just give it up, and go and do something more worthwhile?' Admittedly, our reasons for not doing this are to an extent self-interested, and related to our own careers. But we also see management research as a potentially meaningful and useful activity which enables us to make sense of the world and our place within it. And so in this short book we hope to convince you of the value of management research.

In Search of Management Research

It is thus *possible* to create a tradition that is held together by strict rules, and that is also successful to some extent. But is it *desirable* to support such a tradition to the exclusion of everything else? Should we transfer to it the sole rights for dealing in knowledge, so that any result that has been obtained by other methods is at once ruled out of court? And did scientists ever remain within the boundaries of the traditions they defined in this way? (Paul Feyerabend, 1993: 11, emphasis in original)

This chapter, indeed this whole book, involves trying to understand what management research is and how it is done. The meaning of management research has come to be associated with systematic investigation using scientific methods. We are not opposed to this. But the tools of scientific investigation should simply be a means to an end, not ends in themselves. A parallel can be drawn here with bureaucracy and the notion of goal displacement. When the sociologist Robert Merton (1940) wrote about the bureaucratic personality he had in mind the possibility that bureaucratic forms of organisation could have unintended consequences when organisational rules were followed too literally or interpreted too narrowly. This, he argued, could result in rigid patterns of behaviour, as organisational members became obsessed with procedural compliance in a manner which was ritualistic and didn't necessarily contribute towards the ends that the organisation was supposed to be directed towards. This gives rise to a bureaucratic personality, guided by instrumental rationality and the pursuit of efficiency over and above values.

This relates to the point being made by the philosopher Paul Feyerabend above, when he argues that even if rule-following in scientific research is possible, it may not be desirable because the rationalist principles of the scientific method do not necessarily result in progress. What is more, he argues, the impression that we have of heroes of the scientific revolution, such as Galileo, is a misrepresentation of how these early scientists actually worked (based on rhetorical persuasion as much as empirical evidence). But despite Feyerabend's criticisms, conceptions of research remain founded on these popular stereotypes.

This also gives a clue as to what we think is missing if management research is approached in a way that prioritises the following of strict rules. Because it means that research can become an instrumental, game-playing exercise, without there being a clear sense of why the game is played in the first place. It is this possibility that Grey (2010) has in mind when he talks about the skill and dedication involved in publishing a paper in a high status management journal being similar to that involved in becoming an expert cryptic crossword solver. Consequently, there is a risk that the etymological meaning of research – the activity of searching carefully for something – may be lost. Similar criticisms have been levelled at other social science disciplines, such as Sociology, which Berger (1992) says has succumbed to 'methodological fetishism', or the dominance of methods over content. In this chapter we will explain what is wrong with this approach and consider some alternatives.

Four kinds of management researcher

We think there are four kinds of management researcher. Let's list them:

- *the practitioner-researcher* – this individual seeks out research situations where they can get close to managerial practice. They may appear to have no explicit research agenda, although this can be misleading as there is often a normative intent behind their research, in the sense that it prescribes a solution to a managerial problem. Systematic and scientific methods are seen as a means of enabling the immersion of the researcher in situations involving management practice. For this type of researcher, the purpose of study is often to improve management practice through change.
- *the management theoretician* – this kind of researcher makes theoretical arguments and may build theoretical models. They are sometimes called an armchair researcher, due to their lack of engagement with the empirical world. Their goal is to develop conceptual understandings by drawing on philosophical and social scientific knowledge. They often concentrate on secondary analysis, interpreting empirical research done by others, rather than doing primary research of their own.
- *the craft researcher* – for this type of person research is a creative as well as a technical-rational act; an art as well as a science. This requires not only skill and training but also a sense of imagination and the ability to switch perspectives in order to build up a complex picture of management. It can even involve an element of calculated risk, breaking away from established ways of doing things to enhance the possibility of learning something new.

- *the technical-rational researcher* – for this person the emphasis is on the rigorous use of particular research methods and methodologies, or working with methodological experts, to try to ensure publication in the highest status outlets. They often pursue topics and research designs that are likely to be popular with external funders.

Of course, these are ideal types; most management researchers are a combination of these, and the exact combination of characteristics changes over time. For example, when Richard started working at the shoe factory, he saw himself as a practitioner-researcher. Now towards the end of his career, he sees himself as more of a craft researcher.

There isn't one type of management researcher who is inherently superior to the others. But we do have some misgivings about the technical-rational researcher. This is because we agree with Morgan who says that 'a knowledge of technique needs to be complemented by an appreciation of the nature of research as a distinctively human process through which researchers *make* knowledge' (1983: 7, emphasis in original). Our main focus in this book is therefore on the craft of management research, because we think this is essential in positioning research as a moral, ethical and political (rather than just a technical-rational) activity.

Differences between management research and consultancy

In considering what management research is, we also need to be clear about what distinguishes it from other types of information-seeking and analytical activities like consultancy, or even journalism. Let's start with a famous, or some would say infamous, example of knowledge based on management consultancy. Peters and Waterman's (1982) *In Search of Excellence* is one of the best-selling management books of all time. The authors, who were both management consultants, worked for the firm McKinsey. The book is based on their analysis of a small number of 'excellent' companies which they identified as having a 'strong' culture. In a scholarly critique, Guest (1992) makes a number of points that call into question whether *In Search of Excellence* can be trusted and relied upon as management research.

Peters and Waterman worked with a sample of 75 companies which were all considered to be 'highly regarded' in their industries. However, they rejected 13 of these 75 companies from the category of excellence fairly early on because they failed to represent a model of business that the McKinsey consultants were interested in. Of the remaining 62, they concluded (based on analysis of a range of financial indicators) that 36 were 'excellent'. By 'boosting' the scores awarded for certain factors such as innovation, this number was raised to 43 companies. From their original sample of 75, the McKinsey consultants conducted interviews in around half of them, 21 in companies they judged to be 'excellent', plus another 12 which they deemed to be 'near misses' using their criteria for excellence. However, they only spoke to senior executives within these firms as well as outside commentators like business journalists.

There are numerous problems with this approach. First, it was not a representative sample of the employees in these organisations. Speaking to lower-level employees would probably have provided an interesting complementary perspective. This might have challenged some of the rather self-congratulatory assertions made by senior people in the firms, who said things like: the CEO 'praised initiative and staff skill' and 'rewarded innovation'. The *ad hoc* nature of the sample used by the McKinsey consultants meant that they may have omitted organisations that would have qualified at the outset. It is also questionable whether some of the qualifying attributes employed in the study, such as 'innovation', can be measured objectively. In addition, the authors 'boosted' the value of certain attributes, with little explanation, in order to make the sample bigger. Guest concludes that the whole process on which Peters and Waterman based their book lacked a methodology. In short, *In Search of Excellence* is not management research in any meaningful sense of the term.

So while the McKinsey consultants were searching for excellent management, they failed to base this on excellent research. This contradicts the view of Gummesson (2000) who argues that there isn't really much difference between a management consultant and a management researcher. Gummesson uses the metaphor of a pecking and defecating bird to represent both of these activities. The only significant difference between them is that the management researcher pecks at small aspects of managerial practice and contributes voluminously to theory, whereas the consultant pecks at a small amount of theory and contributes voluminously to managerial practice. For Gummesson, it is just a difference of degree.

According to Gummesson's logic, we might argue that managers, as well as consultants, often do research as part of their jobs; they collect data, analyse it and use it to draw conclusions. But the purposes that this activity is directed towards vary considerably. For example, Richard was once asked by ICI to do some research into how managers in the company made strategic decisions. They wanted him to use a qualitative research method which involved asking managers to keep diaries where they recorded their daily activities. Richard was keen on this as he had used this method in previous research. He encouraged the managers to record their activities in detail – including time spent walking about the factory or discussing things over coffee. But as the study progressed it became clear that the research formed part of an initiative that managers were using to improve efficiency, and the data was going to be used as a rationale for cutting out 'time wasting' activities such as coffee breaks. Richard also realised that the senior team commissioning the study was unaware of previous management research, such as the study by Mintzberg (1973), which also used a diary method to study what chief executives do in their day-to-day lives. Crucially, Mintzberg found that tours of the work site or time spent talking with colleagues in corridors was of high value in enabling senior managers to gather information quickly that enabled them to make decisions and deal with the fragmented nature of their work roles.

It can often be the case that management research has already been done which, if known about, helps make sense of a current situation. Recall the accident in 2010 involving 33 Chilean miners trapped for 69 days 2,300 feet below ground in a copper mine before eventually being rescued. The men waited for 17 days after the huge landslide before any of the rescue team even made contact with them, eating just a teaspoon of tuna and drinking a few sips of milk each day to make their rations last longer. At this point, as far as the trapped miners were concerned, especially given the poor safety record of the mining company that employed them, they could not be sure anyone was seriously looking for them. And yet as the first grainy camera images of the men singing for the cameras emerged from the mine, they explained that they had tried to keep 'everything organised', by forming routines for games, prayer, and allocating different roles to individuals.

While recognising their undoubted bravery, we should not be too surprised at this. In 1958 a researcher named Donald Roy published an article documenting the social organisation of time based on his undercover study of a small group of factory operators. He called his article 'banana time', a phrase used by the workers to describe the ritual breaks they had devised to deal with the formidable 'beast of monotony' caused by the extreme repetition and tedium of the tasks they were employed to do. Roy's point was that it wasn't managers who ensured the social and psychological well-being of the workers, but the workers themselves, by organising themselves in ways that involved humour to punctuate their working day. Although the conditions faced by the Chilean miners were undoubtedly more extreme, Roy's study helps us to understand how workers cope with difficult conditions by establishing predictable patterns of social behaviour.

Similarly, when the scandal broke in 2004 revealing the abuse of detainees by US military police at the Abu Ghraib prison in Iraq, many commentators drew parallels with a study conducted by Zimbardo and his colleagues in the 1970s. Zimbardo's research involved an experiment (Haney et al., 1973) to see how people responded to pressures to conform in situations that resembled 'total institutions' (Goffman, 1961), where people are set apart from the outside world and all treated in the same way together.

The tendency to forget research that can help us to make sense of current managerial situations is a reflection of 'presentism', where 'the present is often assumed to be a period of unprecedented change, heralding the dawning of a new age' (Booth and Rowlinson, 2006: 6). We have noticed that students have a tendency to think that any management research which is more than ten years old is by definition 'out of date' and thus irrelevant, a situation that would be unimaginable in some other academic disciplines like politics or history. This is problematic in a number of respects, not least because there is a risk of reinventing the wheel, through conducting a study which simply repeats what has already been done before, perhaps without even realising it, and interpreting the data in a way which does not acknowledge the findings of previous studies. Burrell (1997) puts this down to the obsession with recency which is combined, among other things, with the desire for relevance, a theme we return to in Chapter 2.

A further problem arises when the management consultant or organisation that has commissioned the study has a strongly favoured outcome which they hope will arise from it. A recent illustration of this can be found in the UK TV series *The Apprentice*, where one of the candidates carried out what she called 'consumer research', by asking travellers on the Paris Metro questions about car usage to establish whether there was a market for a new car product. Despite the emphatic responses of Parisians that they were a city of car users and the product was a good one, she reported back to her team that people were not in favour of it because *she* didn't think the seat was very saleable. As this rather extreme example shows, researchers who are involved in the practice of management sometimes allow this to cloud their interpretation of data.

The way in which consultants and academic researchers engage with theory is also different. Management researchers are more focused on description (what is), whereas management consultants tend to be more interested in prescription (what should be done). Consultants are therefore more likely to apply normative theory. Like technical-rational researchers, they are also more likely to have an instrumental rather than an intrinsic approach to the value of theory. Consequently, consultants and managers tend to approach research in a way that is more instrumental and solution-focused than management researchers. Theory is often interpreted relatively narrowly or not at all, and there is sometimes an element of crude empiricism, wherein research is seen simply as a means of presenting neutral facts.

But as our 'practitioner-researcher' category illustrates, some management researchers adopt an approach that is closely related to consultancy. In supervising students doing dissertation projects, we have noticed that many of them struggle to identify with the idea of being a researcher and sometimes fall back on an identity based on consultancy. This frames how they think of research questions and encourages them to approach them in a managerialist way, rather than being critical and analytical. It is also problematic because they fill the dissertation with bullet point recommendations, as though it was a business or management report to be submitted to a client or a line manager. Recommending a particular course of action to solve a problem is not the main point of research writing, although this may come later. Instead the primary purpose is to understand what is going on.

Differences between management research and journalism

So what is the difference between journalism and management research? In the 1970s, Studs Terkel wrote a book called *Working: People Talk About What They Do All Day and How They Feel About What They Do*. Terkel, who was from Chicago, was a journalist, a radio presenter, a novelist and an oral historian. He was also an expert in getting people to tell their stories. Key to this was his skill in listening, giving people the time and space in which to talk about their experiences. In the book he presents a series of first-person accounts. Such stories are referred to in research as vignettes. The stories were based on interviews he carried out in which he asked people to talk about their working lives. Stories were told by American men and women who did all kinds of work, from a policeman to an airline stewardess, a supermarket checker and a plant manager. They illustrated the mundane experience of work and the importance of routine for the people who did them.

To take another example, in 2001 American journalist Barbara Ehrenreich wrote a book called *Nickel and Dimed: On (Not) Getting By in America*, based on her attempt to gain low-wage, low-skill employment in companies like *WalMart*. Five years later she published another book, this time about white-collar, managerial work. In both cases, she didn't tell her prospective employers that she was a journalist doing research for a book. In management research we refer to this as covert study, because the people being studied don't know the person they're speaking to is a researcher. We would describe Ehrenreich's research as participant observation, because the researcher is seeking to understand the social phenomenon they are interested in by participating directly in the setting, rather than observing it from a distance. Both of these techniques were also used by Donald Roy (1958), mentioned earlier.

However, neither Terkel's nor Ehrenreich's books would be seen as management research, and nor would the authors describe themselves as management researchers. The reasons for this are complex and some of these distinctions might seem relatively pedantic. The first relates to conventions entailed in creating knowledge. In management research there is an expectation that the researcher gives an explicit account of how they conducted the research and how they analysed the data collected. This involves providing the reader with information about the people or situations that constitute the focus of study and showing how this is related to an existing body of knowledge about the subject. To do this, the researcher must demonstrate their understanding of existing knowledge, usually by reviewing the accumulated research literature. They need to cite this literature, providing a set of references that enables the reader to go and access this published work for themselves.

Researchers also need to demonstrate an understanding of the principles of knowledge creation, including what knowledge is and how it is generated. These are termed epistemological issues. They also need to consider the reality status of their subject of study – whether it is something that has an objectively real existence or is dynamically constituted through the actions and perceptions of the people who engage with it. This is an ontological issue. Researchers must also show skill in use of research methods. They must also demonstrate that they understand how the quality of research is assessed. This includes awareness of notions of 'good practice' established over time, and how these sensibilities have changed (so that certain research practices which might once have been considered acceptable, like covert research, are now rarely considered ethically acceptable).

Neither Ehrenreich nor Terkel do these things. What is more, the publication of their work is not reliant on any form of peer evaluation. This is the process whereby research is reviewed by other management researchers, who decide whether or not it is good enough to be published. Instead, Ehrenreich and Terkel rely on the judgements of publishers, who determine whether or not there is an audience for their work, and on readers, who decide whether or not they find the work meaningful and interesting. You might be thinking that management research *should* be evaluated like this. And you might have a point. After all, why shouldn't management research be evaluated according to whether people find it interesting and consider it worth taking the time to read and think about it?

Physics envy in management research

To explain why these are not the primary criteria used to define management research we must turn to a particular affliction that management researchers tend to suffer from, popularly referred to as physics envy (Thomas and Wilson, 2011), so named because it involves a degree of anxious comparison. Physics envy is a term used by those who are critical of the emulation of positivist methods associated with natural or 'hard' sciences[1] like physics.

According to the positivist tradition of knowledge creation, research is a neutral, value-free enterprise, in which researchers go about collecting objective data through empirical observation. This is called phenomenalism. Positivist researchers approach their research subject by reviewing existing knowledge and using this to generate hypotheses, which they seek to test empirically. If a hypothesis is rejected, the theory must be modified. This is known as a deductive approach to theory building. The purpose of this hypothetico-deductive method is to generate law-like theory that applies independently of time and place – known as nomothetic knowledge. The goal for positivist researchers is to generate knowledge about management that enables explanation of how and why things are as they are, and through this to influence the future.

The positivist tradition has profound implications for the way management researchers see themselves in relation to their subject of study. If you were asked to picture a typical scientist, the image conjured up might be of a bespectacled man or woman wearing a white lab coat, perhaps examining something through a microscope, maybe carrying a clipboard – the dispassionate, neutral observer who studies her subject from a distance. This stereotype reflects an *etic* view of research, a 'fly on the wall' or outsider perspective. It assumes that the phenomenon being studied exists independently of the person who studies it. It also assumes that the researcher can reach an understanding of the phenomenon they are interested in by studying it from a distance. What is more, this distance is seen as desirable because without it there is a danger that the researcher will affect their subject of study by studying it, thereby invalidating their findings.

Yet very little management research has resulted in the kind of explanatory, generalisable knowledge that positivist researchers aspire to create. A further problem with this approach is that it assumes it is possible to generate management theory that is neutral, detached and free from value-judgement. This is a highly problematic assumption, for reasons which will become clear later. Plus, in contrast to the natural sciences, and in common with many social science and humanities disciplines, management research is characterised by so-called 'soft' knowledge, based on recursive development, the same issues being returned to over and over again. It is also characterised by a lack of consensus surrounding what questions should be asked and what constitutes respectable or legitimate knowledge. The affliction of physics envy is therefore crucial in understanding the ideas about scientific knowledge upon which some management research is based.

The interpretive other

There is another group of management researchers who go by the label interpretivists, or sometimes social constructionists, who claim that the study of social systems is not amenable to exploration using methods and standards traditionally associated with the natural sciences. If we had to imagine what this type of researcher would look like we might think of someone who is less 'buttoned up' and more casually dressed, wearing jeans or even, as Learmonth and Humphreys (2011) observe, shorts and sandals to work, perhaps having a slightly hippyish style about them, as though they came of age in the 1960s and 1970s. This is not that surprising because a significant growth of the interpretive research tradition in the social sciences[2] can be linked to currents that flourished in these countercultural decades which fostered a willingness to question established ways of doing things and to experiment with alternatives. This built on an earlier era of interpretivism, in the form of the Chicago School, a group of US based sociologists who were committed to developing naturalistic ways of studying social life based on detailed, qualitative investigation, partly a reaction to the positivist tradition which was particularly dominant in the early part of the twentieth century in this discipline. The interpretive researcher might therefore be characterised as something of a rebel in contrast to the dominant positivist tradition.

Interpretivists would suggest that it is very difficult, if not impossible, to generate nomothetic knowledge in relation to complex domains of human activity like management because they are so dependent on the social actors who are involved in them for the meanings that are generated. They would further argue that management knowledge is situationally specific, owing to the complexities and the unique character of the particular cultural and historical moment that is being studied, and therefore not able to be generalised from, except in the most tentative and thought-provoking ways which cannot form the basis for changing organisational behaviour or making managerial decisions. This is known as ideographic knowledge.

The goal of this type of researcher is therefore to generate understanding through knowledge creation. They don't approach their research subject by generating hypotheses in relation to it. Instead they use existing literature on the subject to form a research question which they take into the fieldwork setting, and adjust or adapt depending on the themes and findings that emerge during data collection. We call this an inductive and iterative (cyclical) approach to theory building. Interpretive researchers argue that in order to understand management, we need to get close to the people who are affected by it. They therefore adopt an *emic* or 'experience-near' approach to study (Geertz, 1974), whereby management is understood from an insider perspective. Consequently, the researcher gets involved with the people they study, possibly even affecting outcomes and events through their presence.

Of course, these portrayals are crude oversimplifications which cannot do justice to the diverse array of practices and people that exist within and outside these traditions. However, we make no apology for introducing them at this stage because they provide a useful starting point.

Research communities

So now we have a sense of what management researchers look like, the next question is where and how do you find them? Geertz (1974) suggested that if you want to understand a field of scholarship, you need to start by looking at what its members actually do. This is because in order to become established as a field of science, management researchers must develop a shared understanding of what constitutes proper behaviour and what matters in their field of inquiry. Such understandings will be heavily influenced by certain 'leading lights' (Burrell, 1996: 643), scholars who exercise a degree of political influence.

We find it useful to think of management research as a community of practice. To learn how to do management research it is helpful, if not imperative, to become part of this community. In a book which influenced how we understand the process of learning, Lave and Wenger (1991) describe a community of practice as a group that shares certain understandings about what they are doing, including what this means in their lives and for their communities. This provides the basis for learning. Belonging to a social learning system is reliant on three things: first, engagement, by talking to people at conferences or producing artefacts like written papers; second, imagination, in that you have to be able to look in the mirror and 'see' yourself as a management researcher – this involves having some role models with whom you identify; and third, alignment, the feeling that your activities are in line with respected ways of doing things that you perceive to be related to a collective enterprise or shared goal. To join the management research community, you need to establish relationships of mutuality with other members, contributing reciprocally to it as a trusted member, and also to have access to a shared repertoire of language, sensibilities, routines, tools and stories, that enable you to demonstrate your competence (Wenger, 2000). Importantly, participation in a community is experienced as empowering, whereas if you are prevented from participating very much this is a source of powerlessness.

Our own experience illustrates how this works. Around a decade ago Emma was a PhD student supervised by Richard studying payment systems in the chemical industry. She was advised for a while by Tom Lupton, who in the 1950s was one of the first anthropologists in the UK to study managerial systems. Richard's career as a management researcher began ten years prior to that. He was supervised by Angela Bowey, who had been one of Tom Lupton's PhD students. Richard's PhD was also about payment systems.

The point of this story is that management researchers learn their craft from each other, often through the supervision relationship which is similar to an apprenticeship. At times you may think that your supervisor is a God-like figure who has always known how to do research. At other times you may think they are a bit irritating or odd, but you probably won't forget them and they definitely won't forget you. The reasons for this relate to the length and complexity of the process of becoming a management researcher in a community that becomes a bit like an extended (and perhaps dysfunctional) family. We suspect that many other management researchers could tell similar stories about how they learnt their craft.

Sometimes this learning isn't based on a supervision relationship but on knowledge of and respect for the person's research. For example, in the 1970s, management researcher Michael Burawoy did research in the same US factory where Donald Roy carried out his study of output restriction and informal work groups in the 1940s. Burawoy walked along the same corridors, sat in the same offices and may even have spoken to some of the same employees. It seems reasonable to assume that these experiences shaped Burawoy's understanding of what it means to be a management researcher, and that they were more power-ful because he knew that a classic study of organised work had been carried out by a management researcher in the same location 30 years earlier. Interestingly, it was Roy who also inspired Tom Lupton and convinced him in 1955 to set out to test the findings of the earlier Hawthorne studies by observing work practices in a naturalistic setting, rather than under experimental conditions. This resulted in Lupton's book *On the Shop Floor* (1963).

Becoming a management researcher thus positions you as part of a community. Some of the members you know personally, others you do not. This is similar to Bourdieu's (1984) notion of fields, which are distinguished by shared practices and relations between social actors who share a common interest or desire to play certain social games. The process of learning how to do management research is therefore based on socialisation. This is as much about spending time with and talking to other management researchers who hold various forms of profes-sional and educational capital (Bourdieu, 1984), as it is about learning how to do regression analysis or transcribe an interview from a book. In workplaces this is sometimes referred to as 'sitting by Nellie', or more grandly as 'situated learning'. It involves learning how to do a job by watching someone more experienced do it. Seeing how another man-agement researcher interviews a senior manager or negotiates research access has helped us develop our own research practice and experiment with different ways of doing management research.

If you are a newcomer and you want to join the management research community, you learn the rules by participating in the group's shared socio-cultural practices.[3] One way of doing this is by participat-ing in a gathering of management researchers, such as an academic conference, where you will see old-timers in action (so to speak), pre-senting papers and conducting themselves in ways that reveal to you their particular values and attitudes.

As you might imagine, management research is not one big unified community of practice, but rather a series of smaller communities, many of which have quite distinct practices. For example, the Critical Manage-ment Studies community, which has its own research gatherings, displays certain cultural rituals of behaviour and practice which reflect a kind of masculine, critical, rebellious identity, for example by favouring drinking rituals and eschewing the suit-and-tie presentation of a 'businesslike' self (Bell and King, 2010). A sharply observed article by Ford and Harding (2008) suggests the kinds of behaviours one sees at conferences provide a means whereby a small number of powerful people dominate a large number of others. This is achieved through infantilisation, for example by speaking to them as if they were children, but also through seduction, as important speakers parade themselves before their audience, stroking their hair and wearing smart suits. The point of all of this is to say that you can learn a lot about a community by observing how its members behave at public events like this where they give what Goffman (1959) calls 'frontstage' performances.

The importance of understanding how to become part of a research community applies to undergraduate, Masters and MBA students doing a small research project, as well as PhD students and business school lecturers and professors. But being apprenticed into a community is often characterised by asymmetrical power relations. The apprentice is often heavily dependent on their supervisor not only for advice and guidance but also to confer legitimacy upon them and give them access to contexts where they can participate in community activities.

But there are alternative ways of learning how to become a management researcher. Under conditions of what Lave and Wenger (1991: 93) describe as benign neglect, groups of novitiates can organise their learning among themselves, such as by meeting up informally to talk about their research. This can make them less isolated and more mutually supporting. It provides an alternative to the master–apprentice model of research supervision which is rather paternalistic, and can be experienced as disappointing and frustrating, especially if the student ends up pressured to pursue research avenues that align with their supervisor's research identity, rather than their own (Jones, 1995).

Communities in conversation

To learn how to do management research, one of the first things you need to do is to engage in conversation with people who are doing it. Reading a book about management research, such as this one, is all very well, but you also need to join a community of management researchers so that you can have conversations about research. This might sound rather grand, perhaps conjuring up images of men with beards and bald heads sitting smoking pipes in deep leather armchairs in a book-filled room exchanging intellectual ideas. Whereas, in fact, some of the best research conversations we have ever had have been in rather unlikely and uninspiring places, such as drab university coffee lounges or on long train journeys.

Huff (1999) describes management research as a conversation based on ongoing dialogue that takes place in the classroom, at conferences, by email, or perhaps nowadays on Skype or Twitter. It involves newcomers as well as experienced researchers from different universities and different parts of the world. But the most important aspect of the conversation takes place in published work – in journals, books, and their electronic equivalents. If you want to participate in the research conversation, Huff recommends that you write. Writing is not just a way of communicating findings, it also enables you to understand how scholarship works, including what Huff (1999: 5) calls the 'tacit norms and subtle nuances that characterize good scholarship'. Important questions to ask are: 'what conversations do I want to participate in?' and 'what audiences do I want to reach through my research?' Huff even suggests that you imagine yourself having conversations with researchers in your community so you get used to the idea that you might have something to add. She also gives advice based on the rules of normal conversation which is helpful in considering how to frame your contribution to the conversation, in a way that others are likely to respect:

1 *listen before you speak* – don't pile in without having listened to (i.e. read) the work of other conversationalists;
2 *connect with points already made* – don't try and change the track of the conversation onto something you are interested in; instead make an effort to connect to what others are saying;
3 *be interesting* – be clear, concise, try to avoid saying something that they already know;
4 *be polite* – the desire to be noticed can push you towards bravado or even aggression, try to resist this, it is not good conversational practice. (Huff, 1999: 47)

The bottom line is that you are unlikely to be listened to (i.e. published) if you are talking to yourself. Similar conversational practices have been noticed in other kinds of problem-solving work, such as that done by photocopier technicians who, as organisational ethnographer Julian Orr (1996) observed, spend a great deal of time telling stories to one another about the process of fixing machines.

Research communities as material, virtual and textual

Increasingly, communities of management researchers are virtual rather than actual, gathering in cyberspace via websites, discussion forums and listservs, rather than on a university campus. Virtual communities of practice also often have the advantage of being very international, and participation is not reliant on having the funds to be able to travel to far-flung destinations.

An example relates to the field of strategy research, which has traditionally been dominated by a small handful of strongly positivist-oriented publications such as *Strategic Management Journal*. Since the turn of the millennium, however, there has been something of a shift with the development of a community oriented towards the study of what is termed 'strategy-as-practice'. This forms part of a broader interest in the so-called 'practice turn' in social theory, which has led researchers to turn their attention to the processes through which management and organisations are constituted on an ongoing basis. In the case of strategy-as-practice, this has opened up spaces for more interpretive research.

By forming a management research community, comprising several prominent as well as some less well-known management researchers, starting in 2003 members began to set an agenda, by publishing several 'special issues' about strategy-as-practice in high-status journals like *Long Range Planning* and *Journal of Management Studies*. They also ran regular streams, tracks, symposia and workshops at leading management research conferences, the proceedings of which are often published electronically. This helped to encourage established researchers and doctoral students from related fields to explore and identify with the strategy-as-practice community and orient their research in ways that related to it. One of the most innovative things this community did was to establish a website which acts as a resource repository and a discussion space for researchers, listing recently published articles in the field. The site name was later changed to the Strategy as Practice International Network, reflecting the community's growing international membership. They also published several handbooks or edited collections with prestigious academic publishers like Cambridge University Press, which gave a comprehensive overview and mapped the current progress of the field (e.g. Golsorkhi et al., 2010). In a fairly short space of time, through developing a strong identity, a successful and relatively influential research community was constructed.

As this example shows, one of the most important means through which particular management research communities are constructed involves researchers committing their thoughts to print. This constitutes a way of saying 'this is the direction that management research is going in and we think it overlooks [x] and therefore we have published this handbook or started that new journal to try to redress this imbalance and reflect the growing interest in this emerging and important area. Through this new journal/book we will endeavour to take management research in a new, interesting and potentially more worthwhile direction'. This is what organisational aesthetics researchers have recently done, by setting up their own online journal.[4] As these examples show, management research communities are thus material (in the form of getting together through events such as conferences and workshops), virtual (forming communities through online forums and networks) and textual (creating groups of like-minded management researchers through publishing activities).

◖▬▬▬◗ Communities that remember – or forget

The management research community can also be understood as mnemonic, a group that develops a commonly shared understanding of the past (Rowlinson et al., 2010). According to this view, the collective memory of the management research community is constructed by expressing attitudes toward the past and attaching meaning to them. One of the things we hope to do in this book is to provide a focus for remembering, rather than forgetting the past as a basis from which to form identities in the present. We do this mainly by telling stories. We think this provides a valuable counterweight to the prescriptive tone sometimes associated with methods textbooks, showing the foundations of the field to be built on methods that rarely follow a normative, 'best practice' model of research design. It also helps to demonstrate the historical contingency of management research, as specific to the time and place in which it is done.

Take the case of Melville Dalton, a Chicago School trained industrial sociologist and author of the classic study of informal organisation and unofficial reward, *Men Who Manage* (1959). Emma has argued that the intensive, ethnographic research done by Dalton (who took jobs in the organisations he studied and spent a number of years researching them), could not be carried out in the same way today (Bell, 2011). This is in part because the methods Dalton used would not be considered respectable in today's climate. Dalton argued that it was impossible to study unofficial action other than by using covert methods which enable the researcher to get sufficiently close to the subject. But this argument would not cut much ice with a university ethics committee today. One reason why management researchers do not tend to remember their collective past is because the reality of management research is often messier, more complex and contingent than the community is inclined to admit. Added to this, the demand for scientific rigour in publishing, means that 'warts and all' methodological accounts tend to get written out of published articles.

Conclusion

In this chapter we have introduced four different kinds of management researchers. We have been careful to point out the strengths and weaknesses associated with each of these types, and to show that in practice, researchers often take on identities that combine elements from all of them. One reason for introducing these different types is to encourage you to think about what kind of researcher you want to be.

Becoming a management researcher relies on a process of socialisation through which you become part of a community and develop an identity as a researcher. This can be a strong community, within which you participate fully, or you can be an occasional member of several communities, engaging with each more casually. But not everyone becomes a full participant, and the process of trying to join a community can sometimes be experienced as quite isolating, socially as well as intellectually.

We have also suggested that, contrary to accounts that emphasise the systematic and scientific nature of research as a planned process, management research is often a messy, unpredictable and politicised process which does not readily lend itself to stereotypical ideals of objective neutrality. This is a theme we will return to again and again. And yet we are not advocating the abandonment of all attempts to pursue systematic, scientific management research, but we do think it is important to retain sight of the reasons why management researchers do what they do. In other words, there is a need to search for the purpose of management research, rather than unquestioningly accept conventions surrounding the production of management knowledge, without asking why they exist in the first place.

Notes

1   So called because they generate hard knowledge, which has well established criteria for judging claims to new knowledge, and is characterised by steady, cumulative growth.
2   Marked by publications like the influential *Sage Handbook of Qualitative Research,* first edited by Denzin and Lincoln in 1994 and now in its fourth edition (2011).
3   This is similar to Becher's (1989) analysis of how academics in various university disciplines saw themselves in relation to their research subjects. Sadly for us, Becher did not include management researchers in his study.
4   http://ojs.wpi.edu/index.php/orgaesthetics/

2

The Purpose of Management Research

> Management research is science's Oliver Twist: a delicate and neglected infant of obscure parentage, it has been suddenly claimed by various competing godfathers for reasons ranging from disinterested charity to commercial exploitation. (Nigel Farrow, 1969: 7)

In this chapter we will discuss why management research is done and the outcomes that derive from it. We focus in particular on two, sometimes conflicting, demands that guide management research. The first is relevance, or the immediate and obvious utility of research to practice. Management research is an applied discipline, like medicine or engineering, where it is generally thought that knowledge produced ought somehow to be useful to practice. Consequently, there is often an implicit or explicit expectation that research will lead directly or indirectly to some kind of action. Many people, including politicians and policymakers, think it is possible and desirable for management research to have this kind of effect.

With global economies currently in a perilous state, few would deny the value of management research making a positive contribution to society. But the effect that management research has on practice is not always positive. If you watched the documentary film *Inside Job* (2010) you will have noticed that it implicates some US and UK based business school researchers in the 2008 global economic and financial collapse. So management research sometimes has a big impact on practice, but not in a way that any of us can necessarily be proud of. To make matters more complicated, evaluating impact is widely acknowledged to be problematic, partly because of the diversity and variety of stakeholders, including governments, private sector companies and trade unions, involved in making such a judgement. We therefore need to ask, relevant to whom and for what purposes (Grey, 2001)?

The second imperative is legitimacy, which is sometimes talked about in terms of its opposite, illegitimacy, as the quote from Farrow at the start of this chapter highlights. By talking about management research as though it were an illegitimate child – with all the social stigma that such a label carries – Farrow highlights the fluidity and relative youth of management studies in universities at the time of writing less than 50 years ago. Academic researchers in other faculties, like economics and sociology, saw management studies as an activity unworthy of scholarly attention. To make the task of management research even harder, business people had little appetite for enabling social scientific study into their activities.

Much has changed since then. The substantial growth in university business and management education has been accompanied by a significant growth in management research, and the development of distinct research sub-disciplines of accounting, marketing, organisation studies, human resource management and tourism, in addition to economics and finance. Substantial financial and cultural investment has been made in management research in this period. Numerous factors now inform debates about relevance and legitimacy, including efforts to measure the impact of management research on economies and societies. This can include relevance (in the sense of having some kind of managerial utility), but it also includes broader assessments of impact, through the building of capacity in societies more generally. This in turn has led to greater differentiation of business schools, with some declaring themselves to be social science schools of management that aim to develop a reflective, critical approach to teaching and research, while others brand themselves as providers of a professional training to equip managers with the skills and knowledge required for practice (Ferlie et al., 2010).

Much debate has been waged over the purpose of management research, often in the pages of management journals like the *Academy of Management Review*, *Academy of Management Learning & Education*, *Academy of Management Perspectives*, *Journal of Management Studies* and *British Journal of Management*, which every couple of years or so publish collections of papers in which eminent management researchers offer their views. A key issue concerns the relationship between research and practice. Should management research lead to developments in academic theory, or should research result in finding solutions to practical managerial problems? And if the aim is to produce practical knowledge that can be used by managers, how do we ensure that the knowledge that is produced is communicated in a way that enables managers to use it? These preoccupations have come to be known as the theory–practice gap.

What makes management research different?

To engage with these issues we first need to understand what makes management research different, in comparison to research in other social science disciplines. Several decades ago a typology was developed by psychologist Anthony Biglan (1973) which he used to map how researchers in all disciplines saw their field of scholarship. The framework distinguished between 'hard' versus 'soft' disciplines and those that are 'pure' versus those that are 'applied'. Biglan's original schema was later extended by Becher (1989) to incorporate the social-organisation dimension of disciplines, which Becher argued were either 'convergent' (tightly knit groups of researchers who share a common purpose) or 'divergent' (a fragmented grouping where there is little shared identity). He also suggested that disciplines were either 'urban' (comprised of researchers who are clustered densely together in addressing a set of issues, as in a city), or 'rural' (metaphorically ploughing their own fields, many miles away from their neighbours).

This typology was later taken up by management researchers (Tranfield and Starkey, 1998), who said management research is a relatively soft, applied discipline that has divergent characteristics and is rural in nature. They went on to say that theoretical concepts about manage-ment must be developed in the context of application and argued that knowledge produced in this emergent way could give rise to more rel-evant theory. They therefore recommended management researchers work more closely with users, so the diffusion of knowledge could include those who have participated in the knowledge-production pro-cess. Through this process of interaction and engagement, they sug-gested practitioners could become more reflective and critically aware, and knowledge could be transferred tacitly rather than in codified form.

Debates about the nature of managerial knowledge production were further extended through the work of Gibbons et al. (1994), who describe two kinds of research. Mode 1 characterises the traditional approach to research in which knowledge generation occurs within the context of existing institutions and academic disciplines. This approach is driven by the academic community's agenda, and its legitimacy arises from the disciplinary perspective taken. The work produced is judged to be of quality by academic peers and, as a consequence, knowledge is hierarchical and incremental. The dissemination of knowledge occurs downstream of its production with little immediate concern for its practical implications. Mode 2, on the other hand, is research charac-terised by the production of knowledge in the context of and through direct engagement with social practice and problems. Definitions of problems are usually application-based, created in a particular context that values the views and perspectives of those involved in practice. As problems in practice are not usually uni-disciplinary, the approach has a transdisciplinary nature as well as valuing tacit understandings of practitioners alongside those of researchers. It emphasises teamwork as opposed to the individual, lone-academic endeavour of mode 1 research, and recognises the transitory nature of knowledge, creating knowledge that can be both produced and exploited almost simultaneously. As a consequence, knowledge becomes more widely shared among various stakeholder groups and the implications of research are considered as important as the findings. Another key aspect of mode 2 knowledge production reported by Tranfield and Starkey (1998) and highlighted by Thorpe and Beasley (2006), is that it occurs as a result of interaction between theory and practice, which is the antithesis of the more traditional mode 1 form, in which theoretical knowledge generally precedes application and where distance is usually maintained between knowledge production and application, as well as between researchers and users. If this kind of system is to work effectively, there must be a rapid interplay between management theory and practice (Tranfield and Starkey, 1998).

Gibbons suggests the process of knowledge transfer can be helped by what he refers to as 'boundary objects', symbolic vehicles that enable people to get together to discuss an issue of shared relevance. Boundary objects involve systems and routines, or individuals that enable the flow of knowledge (as in the Greek agora, a feature of Greek architecture found in most cities where people meet and share information). Gibbons uses an anecdote to illustrate: two individuals who are attracted to each other and wish to get to know each other better but are prevented from doing so without an introduction, by the conventions of their culture. But if they both had dogs, convention would dictate it would be perfectly acceptable for them to discuss their pets and a discussion could easily be started up about, for example, their shiny coats. In this case the dog is the boundary object that brings two individuals together. For management researchers, there is value in thinking about and using boundary objects as a way of making links between research and practice. To give an example from Richard's experience, the Indian company Tata was looking for ways of implementing innovation in its business practices when a senior executive within the firm came across the work of a researcher at London Business School in this area. They worked with the researcher to develop a tool that they could implement in their companies. Through producing this boundary object, the insights of the research were able to be more widely distributed in a way which could influence business practice.

The practical upshot of these classification exercises is to highlight that management problems are impossible to define one-dimensionally. Instead they are almost always an eclectic mix of different issues, each with a number of different dimensions. But there are also similarities between the field of management research and other social science disciplines. The ideas of the process philosopher Alfred North Whitehead (1929) are helpful here. Whitehead sees influence arising from scientific activity as emerging from the capacity to see things anew. In other words, human enquiry is based on having the ability to envisage how the world is and, as a consequence, being able to understand how it might be different (and better) from the way it currently is. This ability to 'see things anew' is what Whitehead considers the basis of good science, irrespective of the field or the discipline. Social science requires researchers to engage in ongoing relationships with the human experiences that form the raw material for the data from which they make sense of the social world they study.

The focus of management research is the problems of managers, their colleagues, and those under the influence of managers, including management researchers themselves. As time passes, the problem studied changes. Because managerial problems are not fixed, universal or entirely tractable, management researchers must try to make sense of them in historical and cultural context. Added to this, it is only by recognising the relationships they have with the phenomena they study that management researchers can understand how to see things anew, in the way that Whitehead outlines. This last point relates to the notion of reflexivity, which we will return to later. For a field like management, seeing things anew according to a process philosophical perspective, involves researchers recognising the intimate relationship between their perspectives and the ongoing problems experienced by people engaged in managing (Thorpe and Holt, 2008).

An impossible goal

In the film *Monty Python and the Holy Grail*, King Arthur of the Britons accompanied by his Knights of the Round Table, is tempted by the lure of the grail, a cup imbued with deep religious significance. In their quest for where it lies, they travel through various lands and face several challenges and hardships. Along the way they are tempted by various interesting diversions. Some fall by the wayside but those who are left stay true to their quest. The film ends abruptly with the remnants of the cast being arrested, having failed to find their holy object. Some might say that the twin imperatives imposed on management researchers – to do research that is relevant to practice *and* perceived as legitimate according to social scientific principles – are doomed to similar failure. This is because the desired goals are in conflict. The question is whether these two imperatives are compatible, or if, as in the quest for the grail, their pursuit is driven by ideological beliefs that are ultimately unrealisable. To understand why this might be the case we have to explore what each of these imperatives means in the context of management research.

Relevance can encourage a trend-spotting attitude towards research, identifying what is currently fashionable in management and then studying it. The idea is that research ought to be of interest to managers and can be used by them to inform and improve their practice. As writers like Huczynski (1993) and Abrahamson (1991) have observed, management is a kind of fashion industry. Management researchers (together with other intermediaries like business media consultants and management gurus), come up with new management ideas, models, maps and frameworks. They disseminate these ideas to managers, through teaching, writing books and other publications, and doing consulting work. Some methods of dissemination are direct (like teaching), while others are indirect – this includes publishing articles in high-quality journals that will, at least initially, only be read by other researchers, before later being disseminated to practitioners. Researchers are usually more involved at the end of the process of introducing new management ideas into organisations, rather than at the beginning or in the middle. Rather than setting agendas, having new ideas and facilitation, all of which is more usually the preserve of consultants, they come in towards the end and play a role in theorising and labelling (Zbaracki, 1998). We might ask ourselves whether this is enough. Perhaps the greatest opportunity to influence practice arises from being involved throughout the process of implementation and in deciding what ideas should be implemented in the first place. This highlights another problem which conspires against the attainment of relevance in management research. This can be explained using Zeno's dilemma, named after the Greek philosopher Zeno, whose views are known through the writings of Aristotle. Zeno's dilemma depicts a hare starting behind a snail and trying unsuccessfully to catch up with it. By the time the hare gets to where the snail was, the snail has moved on. Management research often appears rather like this, with the hare being like the researcher and the manager like the snail.

We also have to consider what is meant by legitimacy in management research. Legitimacy encourages a focus on the quality of research, including whether the scientific methods of research and analysis have been applied rigorously. Shrivastava's (1987) article introduces many broad issues that continue to be debated over 20 years later. He proposes three criteria for evaluating research rigour based on: the conceptual adequacy of the knowledge that guides it, its methodological rigour, and the extent to which empirical findings accumulate into a coherent body of knowledge. He also sets out ways of evaluating the usefulness or relevance of knowledge based on: its meaningfulness to users, the extent to which findings can be translated into concrete actions, its innovativeness, and the cost effectiveness of implementing the findings. Shrivastava's conclusions, relating to the divergence between knowledge creation and practice and the challenges of breadth and fragmentation, provide a precursor to subsequent debates and the extent to which the knowledge creation process has been successful in bridging the perceived gap between rigour and relevance in management research (see for example Fincham and Clark, 2009).

Rigour is a term used in hard sciences like physics, where its application as a value is so consensually widespread that you would not need to say that someone's work was rigorous, because this would be assumed to be the case. In a discipline like sociology, the precise opposite applies; use of terms like bias and rigour are likely to be seen as betraying the researcher's limited understanding of methodological issues, because all research must be biased to some degree (Becher, 1989). In management research, the term rigour is frequently used, but the extent to which it is seen as an appropriate measure of quality, particularly when talking about qualitative research, is contested. Some would argue that other quality measures, such as trustworthiness or authenticity, are more appropriate criteria for evaluating interpretive and post-positivist forms of inquiry that rely on gaining proximity to the research subject.

Concerns about rigour are related to a broader desire among management researchers to achieve scientific legitimacy in the academy. But writers like Bennis and O'Toole (2005) have questioned the constructiveness of this project. They argue that by becoming overly focused on scientific rigour, management researchers have lost touch with managerial practice, which cannot be explained according to scientific principles because it is primarily a profession. Others have suggested management research can be divided into four camps: 'pragmatic' science, which is high in relevance and rigour, and 'pedantic', 'populist' and 'puerile' science which are all lacking to some degree in relevance and rigour (Anderson et al., 2001). They warn that there has been a drift away from pragmatic science in management research that urgently needs to be redressed.

Assessments of legitimacy can also be based on critical distance, or whether the researcher has critically evaluated managerial aims and values. This principle of scholarly neutrality and ideological distance from the subject of study is crucial to the formation of respected scientific disciplines. And yet in management research, the pursuit of relevance potentially undermines the pursuit of critical legitimacy, since the former imperative tends to be performative, focusing on improving management practice rather than critically evaluating it.

The concern to develop a research agenda that is both relevant and legitimate continues to define business schools today, and debates about how a balance might be struck still rage. This tension can be likened to the parable of Buridan's Ass. Buridan's Ass, named after the French philosopher Jean Buridan (1300–1358), starves to death while mid-way between two piles of hay because the simple animal cannot decide which one to choose. The parable is used to denote the impracticality of decision making based on pure reason, especially in a situation involving two equal choices. Management researchers could be seen as facing a similar dilemma between the imperatives of practical relevance and scholarly legitimacy.

Back to the beginning

To understand how these tensions arise, we need to understand how management research began, through the founding of business schools in the United States and Europe.[1] Prior to this, management research did not exist as a distinct and separate scholarly community. When business schools were first introduced in the UK in the mid 1960s, making the connection to managerial practice was seen to be of paramount importance. This was in no small part because most managers at the time could not see the point of management education, believing instead in the 'cult of the amateur' and thinking managers had to be educated in the 'University of Life'. Wilson's (1992) history of Manchester Business School, one of the first in the UK, provides insight into the values and ideals that drove this generation of management researchers. He tells the story of the 'founding fathers' (his term not ours) of Manchester Business School, who searched for 'the Maverick' academic who was willing to work in ways that transcended a single disciplinary approach to address the managerial problems of 'businessmen' (again not our term, but one commonly used at the time). These new business schools used action learning, as more participative and less didactic forms of education that encouraged learning from cases, simulations and role playing, based on work by researchers at the Tavistock Institute (Caswell and Wensley, 2007).

Wilson (1992) also draws attention to the radical insecurities of management researchers in these early days as they sought to reconcile the competing demands of revenue-generating teaching (relevance) with lucrative management consultancy and university demands for high-quality academic research (legitimacy). Some were critical of what they saw as the emergence of an intellectual, 'bookish' culture in the new business schools and sought to redress this by developing an approach to research that had a more technological, problem-solving orientation (Revans, 1982), more akin to departments of engineering. For these people, management research was viewed as a tool that could be used to fix managerial problems. Doctoral study was regarded as an opportunity for management researchers to immerse themselves in the work context and begin to make connections between theory and practice. Many of these early management researchers worked closely with local employers like Pilkingtons and Rolls-Royce on workplace projects that related to current managerial problems and had practical application.

This approach to management research and education works well on a small scale when close interpersonal relationships between researchers and practitioners can be formed. But as business schools, and the demand for undergraduate and postgraduate management education has grown, the challenge has been one of scale, with the danger that meaningful connections between research and practice are not able to be made. Managers benefit most from the kinds of learning and development methods used by early business schools when numbers were small, including action and project-based learning, mentoring and coaching (Fox, 1992). The vast majority of executive education of this kind doesn't actually take place in the business school, but is instead delivered by consultancy companies.[2] The number of practising managers who make use of management research is thus pitifully small. So perhaps we need to rediscover some of the practices developed by these earlier management researchers?

What you measure is what you get

Why does any of this matter to someone starting out as a management researcher today? Doing management research has become a means of building a fairly respectable career, not just for university academics, but also for students, managers and business people who do management research as part of their undergraduate, MBA, specialist Masters, or DBA degree programme. The vast majority of management research takes place in the context of an academic assessment culture which, whatever business schools may say in their publicity, values research publication (especially in high status management journals) above all else. In many cases, management research publishing has become a form of 'gamesmanship' (Macdonald and Kam, 2007), a practice where what is said becomes far less important than where it is published (Willmott, 2011). For many management researchers, the value of their research is measured based on where it is published and this is informed by league tables, journal rankings and citation counts. One of the main problems with audit systems like this as a basis for performance management arises from the fact that they concentrate on what can be measured. The easiest way of measuring management researcher performance is by counting the number of published papers an individual has written. This is much more straightforward than trying to measure whether they have built meaningful relationships with the people they have studied, or whether their research has had an impact on practice.

When Farrow talked of the formation of 'respectable career ladders' (1969: 8) for management researchers, he can hardly have anticipated how important the publishing of journal articles would become, and how this would influence the relationship between relevance and legitimacy. When we talk to management researchers working in business schools in Europe, North America, Australia and New Zealand, we see a consistent pattern. The new generation of management researchers (unlike those of previous generations) have almost all completed a PhD. In their research training, students are increasingly being asked to focus on research rigour. This has the effect of emphasising the technical-rational aspects of doing research, including the use of what is perceived to be the correct methodology.[3] Some talk about this as a game, where the priority is to work on small projects that can be published quickly as papers alongside the PhD, rather than developed over a longer time period.

For the newly recruited lecturer who reaches the next rung of the career ladder, the pace accelerates further, as they are encouraged to specialise even more by engaging with just one specific community of management research practice and publishing off their PhD for several years rather than doing any further empirical work. Research primarily involves working on problems identified in the literature, or those that journal editors identify as priorities. This is what Sandberg and Alvesson (2011) describe as a 'gap spotting' approach to research. It involves identifying a (usually very small) gap in the existing literature and then formulating a research question that attempts to fill it. The problem with this is that most interesting research involves challenging assumptions that underlie existing theory. At this stage in their careers, management researchers are also learning how to teach, and these demands encroach on time available for research. Since rewards in terms of promotion are based almost entirely on research, teaching can quickly come to be seen as a chore and they may try to find ways of doing less teaching, or doing it quickly, so they have more time for research.

Getting onto the next rung of the career ladder relies on publishing papers in the most prestigious business and management journals. An increased amount of energy is therefore given over to playing the publication game. This makes the individual CV (and therefore the management researcher), highly portable, and opens up opportunities to get 'better' jobs in 'better' universities. The transfer market for these 'well-published' individuals is not unlike the transfer market for footballers – both involve fierce competition for 'star' performers who, in exchange for large salaries, are expected to bring in accolades that benefit their employers. But writing papers for prestigious journals takes time and is often undertaken at the expense of engagement with user communities or work related to impact. Even higher up the career ladder, as a senior management researcher, the pressure to publish journal articles does not cease. Ironically, if a management researcher does have an interest in relevance, they usually express this by writing about relevance and publishing it in a prestigious journal!

The politics of publishing

There is a further aspect of these career-building practices that we have not yet mentioned. Spicer (2005) talks about academic 'cartel' building as a means through which members of a particular management research community are required to cite the work of key senior members of that community as a means of gaining entry to it. Citing the work of others is not just a way of demonstrating that you know about existing research, it is also a means of ritualistically affirming membership and identity of a research community (Whitley, 1984), and recognising the scholarly reputation of researchers within it. Such practices may be viewed in one of two ways. A benign interpretation is that this is a way of ensuring that appropriate regard has been paid to existing work in the field. However, a less charitable interpretation would be that it is a cynical attempt to shore up the power of existing researchers through 'normal science', which means that radical or controversial ways of thinking, especially those which are critical of senior members of the community, are less likely to be published, and thus these individuals are silenced, or denied a voice. You may have watched the film *Fight Club* (1999) in which there is the well known line, 'the first rule of Fight Club is: you do not talk about Fight Club'. A version of this has been translated into research circles: 'The first rule of Cite Club is ...' . You get the idea – the intimidatory, hegemonically masculine, identity-stripping (Goffman, 1959), conformity-inducing practices associated with *Fight Club*, are suggested to be applicable in research. It's a depressing thought.

Not only are management researchers involved in practices that restrict the entry of new members into their communities, journal editors too may intentionally try to manipulate the metrics used to evaluate journal performance, such as impact factors (for example by insisting authors who submit new research for potential publication must reference articles that have appeared in the journal in the past). By increasing the impact factor of the journal, editors simultaneously enhance the journal's reputation, the reputation of those who publish in it, and their reputation as a journal editor – making it a win–win situation all round. Added to this, the substantial profits that publishers make from journals (Lilley et al., 2012) are based on publishing research that is often paid for using public funds, in the form of grant funded research, paper writing and editing papers, all of which are done in university time. It therefore seems rather a cheek that university libraries are being forced to cancel subscriptions to some journals due to rapidly rising prices.

As this summary illustrates, the process whereby management research is disseminated through publication in prestigious journals is politicised and is prone to self-interested manipulation. It is therefore highly problematic to make this the sole basis for assessing the worth of management research. It is a sobering fact that 'some 90% of papers that have been published in academic journals are never cited' – in all disciplines (Meho, 2007: 32), and 'as many as 50% of papers are never read by anyone other than their authors, the referees and journal editors'. So legitimacy, if measured in this way, appears to contribute very little to relevance, in the sense of practice-related impact.

Doing research differently

As a consequence of these pressures, management research is becoming instrumental and individualistic. When impact is articulated, it is usually done so in the context of mode 1 study. Performance management has encouraged the pursuit of academic legitimacy at the cost of almost everything else, including engagement and impact. The consequence of expending such a disproportionate amount of effort and placing such high value on research outputs in journals means that publishing becomes the goal rather than what it ought to be – an intermediary stage in the formation of relationships between researchers, practitioners and policymakers, and a stepping stone towards the dissemination of research into practice. The instrumental focus on academic outputs promotes a highly individualised (some might say lonely) style of research that involves little engagement with managerial practice. The role of metrics on management research has thus been to prioritise a particular kind of scientific legitimacy at the expense of relevance.

We therefore need to address the way that management research is organised. All too often this focuses on the individual. To be successful, management researchers need to obtain grant income, write high-quality papers, supervise students (including a quota of PhD students), teach and most probably undertake a number of institutional roles, all at the same time. So what are the alternatives? A more collectivist approach would involve recognising that individual research interests change over time, depending on the person's experience and career stage. It would also involve recognition of non-publication scholarly contributions, like developmental reviewing and administrative roles like conference organising that enable research to be disseminated. Individuals connected to a research team or working in a research centre might concentrate on academic publishing work earlier in their career, in order to gain credibility and develop their standing within a field before taking on teaching and supervising doctoral students. Later in their career, they might take on responsibility for grant income, mentor other staff, and engage with the impact and engagement agendas, freeing earlier career researchers to continue to pursue scholarship. The core idea would be for individuals to be seen as part of a system and for the game to be not simply an individual one. But this would involve greater acknowledgement of the collective responsibility of management researchers to build a culture that supports research. It would involve challenging the dominant logic of scholarly productivity, based on publication in prestigious journals. Instead we might apply the principle of *noblesse oblige*, whereby experienced researchers would be expected to behave honourably, generously and responsibly in helping developing scholars through mentoring and collaboration, in ways that enable them to develop research skills (Northcraft and Tenbrunsel, 2012).

Communities of research generally take a number of years to establish. The characteristics of management research communities have been identified by Harvey and colleagues (2002) as comprising: a clear articulation of strategic direction and leadership; core competence with related diversification; flexible entrepreneurial stance, both intellectual and commercial; a complementary skill mix; thematic organisation; champions to lead the research; good interpersonal relations within the group; and strong internal and external networks. This necessarily includes individuals with a range of interests, who work together and share knowledge. Communities probably need to generate funding, which may be drawn from a number of sources through a wide and well-maintained network of contacts, public as well as private – research councils, policy groups, industrial collaborators, other academic institutions, professional associations and so on. In terms of dissemination, translation and engagement, centres would identify user groups who, in turn, help them to identify their knowledge domains and suitable problems. Publication in journals would still be required, but researchers might also publish in professional journals, newspapers and other media.

Different kinds of knowledge

There is an emerging view in some business schools that it is unsustainable for academic careers to continue to focus solely on published outputs, for professors to negotiate contracts on the basis of no teaching, for management consulting to be carried out privately, and institutional contributions to be made instrumentally. At present, some academic appointments are made solely on the strength of publications alone; the individual may have little experience of PhD supervision, curriculum development or successful knowledge translation. In 1990 the Carnegie Foundation published a report into higher education entitled *Scholarship Reconsidered* (Boyer, 1990). Although the report relates to scholarship as a whole, its recommendations are particularly insightful for management research and the relationship between relevance and legitimacy.

The report discussed the trend towards a singular view of scholarship as research and publication and proposed that the priorities of professors should be enlarged to encompass the integration of knowledge into practice, teaching and service. In the report, Boyer (1990) argues that the debate about teaching versus research needs to give way to a broader understanding of the term scholarship, and an increased recognition of its value. This can also embrace different forms of scholarship, none of which is seen as more important than the other. Scholarship of *discovery* – contributing to the stock of knowledge and the intellectual climate of the university through research and publication – is no more important than the scholarship of *integration*, which gives meaning and context to knowledge. Scholarship of integration also makes connections across disciplines and illuminates data and information for non-specialists. Although closely related to discovery, it reveals itself in what Michael Polanyi refers to as 'overlapping neighbourhoods'. Integration also involves the researcher integrating their own research findings into larger intellectual patterns, and encourages those engaged in the research process to explain exactly what their findings mean. The scholarship of *application* begins the movement to engagement, as the questions asked help the researcher to consider how their work might be applied to problems of consequence.

For some, engagement implies that management researchers need to ask very different questions – for example, enquiring less about how research should influence practice and more about how practice could be influenced by research. Boyer also covers teaching in his argument for scholarship, as it is through teaching that researchers are at their most influential – engaging students and exciting new generations with new possibilities, ideas and perspectives. Teaching can also make researchers more reflective and reflexive (ideas which we will return to later in this book), as they become more conscious of what they know and how this can transform and extend current thinking.

Making a difference

There is no doubt that many management researchers do aspire to address the relevance agenda, and, in so doing, improve the society they live in. Some have suggested that this aspiration is better characterised as 'the management of indifference' (Pettigrew, 2001). Pettigrew uses the example of Thomas More who, shortly before his execution in 1535, suggested that the duty of intellectuals in society is to make a difference. There are two key words here: *duty* and *intellectual*. Duty is something that an academic's conscience would require them to do, whereas defining someone as an intellectual suggests that researchers use rational rather than emotional judgement. Pettigrew suggests that, if management researchers see their ultimate goal as making a difference by doing relevant research, they have a long way to go to realise it. This is due to a number of things. First, not all management researchers agree that research publications should be intermediary goods, a stepping stone towards achieving impact. Instead they hold the view that their priority is 'to produce scholarship for the consumption of their peers, who are usually the only people equipped to understand it and interested enough in it to bother trying'.[4]

Despite this, the desire among management researchers to make their work relevant continues. You only need to read the addresses of past presidents of the Academy of Management, one of the largest global associations of management researchers, to see this concern is deep rooted. Many voice concern over the lack of impact that management research has had on practice and policy. For example, Hambrick (1994) poses the question, 'what if the Academy actually mattered?' Meanwhile, Ann Huff contrasts mode 1 and mode 2 forms of knowledge production and proposes a new category which she labels mode 1½, a compromise position where both theoretical and practical work is required (Huff, 2000). Van de Ven (2007) has for many years advocated the co-production of knowledge, where researchers and practitioners share their constructs and use of rather different research designs from the traditional social sciences. Along the same lines, Bartunek makes a case for collaborative research and Pierce questions the rather limited view of management researchers by asking the question, 'what do we know and how do we really know it?' Ryles asks how we might tackle what he calls the 'great divide' between research and practice, while Rousseau (2006) discusses 'evidence-based management'. This technique, imported from medical research, is suggested to provide a methodology for translating knowledge based on the best or strongest evidence into managerial practice. It involves systematically reviewing all the available knowledge concerning a particular problem or issue and translating it into a form that is relevant to practitioners. Critics of evidence-based management argue that the proposed neutrality of these concerns is misleading and tends to focus on knowledge producers as the problem without considering the difficulties that arise from the ways in which practitioners engage with knowledge (Weick, 2001).

Handwringing about the legitimacy and relevance of management research goes beyond the management research community. Recently, Richard was interviewed for a senior research-related position. The interview panel was made up of people who were not management researchers. The first question they asked him focused on the extent to which management research might assist government in implementing cuts in public sector funding while retaining morale and effectiveness. Another question probed the extent to which management research might help government develop policy in areas relating to the national and global economy, such as potential food shortages caused by climate change and reducing carbon emissions while retaining economic performance. Yet another addressed the extent to which academic researchers were engaged with practice and how such interaction might be practically improved. On another occasion, Richard was attending a meeting at the offices of the UK Department for Business, Innovation and Skills to discuss the metrics used to measure researcher performance and their effects on the behaviour of researchers in business schools. The person chairing the meeting asked the group of management researchers how business schools might help support the economic recovery and in what ways they might use their skills and expertise to help small and medium-sized enterprises, which are seen by politicians as the power-house for innovation and wealth creation. As these stories show, concerns about the relevance and legitimacy of management research extend far beyond the boundaries of the field.

At a global level, there have been a number of high-profile statements of the challenges facing humanity, such as the United Nations Millennium Development Goals and the Copenhagen Consensus that may affect attitudes towards management research in the future. These have begun to influence the policies of government bodies with responsibility for research. In the UK the mechanism for allocating state funding for research is via the research councils; in many other countries there are similar organisations or government bodies that fulfil this task. These agencies encourage engagement with practice and policy, they also encourage interdisciplinary research. Overall, there is a feeling that the most challenging research questions faced today, related for example to global economic performance, health and well-being, new technology and innovation, environment, energy, population dynamics, security and justice, require interdisciplinary research teams working across boundaries. We think there is a role for management research in this broad project.

Conclusion

In this chapter we have focused on the tension between legitimacy and relevance, two imperatives that have had a profound influence on management research. In tracing the reasons for the tension between them we have focused on issues relating to the purpose of management research and the translation of academic research into practice. We have also looked at the requirement for management research to be conducted in a way that is considered scientifically legitimate.

Some argue that the world of academia and the world of management practice are incommensurable, each having developed different languages, methodologies and practices that make them distinct. Perhaps the gap between them is now impossible to bridge. All too often, when practitioners are asked to read research articles, they say that they are too academic and theoretical. Links to practice in published work are not always made explicit, let alone communicated. So often, what we know is constrained and shaped by views of what counts as scientifically rigorous, and these views are very firmly embedded in the practice and traditions of academic research. Many management researchers have built successful careers by employing these approaches, and are reluctant to change. This can limit possibilities for developing innovative research designs and on many occasions prevents the kind of interactions that might generate context-sensitive, meaningful knowledge (Thorpe and Holt, 2008).

Added to this, little interaction takes place between researchers and practitioners through which findings may be translated into practice. When groups like management consultants do take academic research and repackage it in a way which makes it more comprehensible to different stakeholder groups, it is often found to be useful. But this relies on strong relationships between researchers, consultants and practitioners, each group valuing the different knowledge and skills that the other brings to the process. Yet retaining a high degree of separation between research and practice is in our view no longer viable when management research is needed to understand and address pressing organisational problems, including those that led to the current global economic crisis.

Much of what we have discussed in this chapter has implications for research training, specifically of PhD students, many of whom in our experience have little awareness of impact. The majority of doctoral students, by the end of their first year of studies, have strong views about how research should be conducted. These views, which are significantly influenced by their supervisors, shape their perspective on what counts as management research.

Failure to challenge the culture of performativity in management research makes us complicit in constructing research value solely on the basis of journal lists. The game we signal as important is one that sees the value of management research as based on generating small-scale insights into phenomena and publishing them as papers in prestigious journals. This relies on a failure to question whether the research that gets published in these journals really is so much better. Starbuck's (2005) conclusion, based on statistical analysis of publishing patterns in prestigious journals, is that editorial selection involves considerable randomness. Consequently, some very good research gets rejected by high-status journals and some less prestigious journals publish excellent research.

We therefore need to focus on the value and purpose of management research rather than the pursuit of narrow, self-interested goals. Management research has long been plagued by accusations of a 'greed culture' (Wilson, 1992: 101), where the desire for long-term research is compromised by short-term lucrative opportunities for personal and professional gain. This makes the question of purpose all the more important, since without it, it is impossible to navigate the complex and sometimes contradictory imperatives that management researchers face.

Notes

1 Grey's (2009) book in this series contains an excellent analysis of the history of the business school, including its political and cultural significance.
2 This was a finding of the UK ESCRC Advanced Institute of Management (AIM).
3 For example, structural equation modelling is perceived to be increasingly in demand in high status journals.
4 James Ladyman (2009) writing in the *Times Higher Educational Supplement*.

Philosophies of
Management Knowledge

> From the perspective of those engaged in its creation, knowledge
> would appear more closely comparable with a badly made patch-
> work quilt, some of whose constituent scraps of material are only
> loosely tacked together, while others untidily overlap, and yet others
> seem inadvertently to have been omitted, leaving large and shapeless
> gaps in the fabric of the whole. (Tony Becher, 1989: 7)

> Philosophical ideas do not necessarily lead to methodological ones
> or precede them in the timeline of a researcher's analytic or theo-
> retical development. (Dvora Yanow and Peregrine Schwartz-Shea,
> 2006: xii)

Why is it important to talk about philosophies of knowledge in a book
about management research? Quite simply, because beliefs about how
knowledge is created provide the foundations from which we decide what
questions to ask and how to go about finding answers to them. These
concerns focus on the nature of knowledge. They apply to all areas of
social scientific research and researchers in other disciplines also see them
as important. But here we are concerned with how particular theoretical
traditions are expressed and enacted in management research, which can
be quite different from the way they are understood by historians or geog-
raphers. This is the point being made by Becher in the quote above. He
suggests that the differences between different academic disciplines
(Becher calls them tribes) in their approach to knowledge creation are so
great that research doesn't resemble a neatly woven whole, but instead a
patchwork comprised of very different materials.

If you are reading this because you have to write a thesis or a dissertation you might be tempted to skip this chapter, thinking that this
philosophical stuff is only for full-time researchers with jobs in universities to pontificate about. There are two reasons why you should stick
with it. First, as we have already said, we hope you will become educated users of management knowledge, so you can evaluate a study for
yourself, rather than be forced to rely on someone else's interpretation
of it. When you read an article or book that presents someone's research

findings, you need to have a sense of where the writer is coming from in terms of their epistemological stance. And herein lies an important point – EVERY management researcher makes epistemological assumptions, whether or not they are up front in telling you this in their published work or not.

Second, if you are doing research yourself, you need to come up with a label that you can use to describe what you are doing, one that indicates the theoretical commitments that you hold about the nature of the knowledge you have generated through your research project. You also need to show how you did the research, and to show that your methods of data collection and interpretation are consistent with your epistemological stance. This is important. It is not very convincing to say that you are an interpretive researcher who wants to understand management through the eyes of the people involved in it, if your research design involves you emailing a group of potential respondents a closed-response questionnaire and you analyse the data using SPSS. This is because you have not made an attempt to gain insight into their views about management. Instead you have imposed a particular conception of the relevant issues based on your understanding (which has probably been derived from previous research and your own experience). To an extent, this is unavoidable. Most management researchers acknowledge that research is inevitably guided by *a priori* assumptions, often based on existing theory or belief. Apart perhaps from some advocates of grounded theory (more on this later), who encourage 'the initiation of research without any preconceived theoretical ideas about the topic being researched' (Layder, 1993: 19).

Either way, your research will be stronger if you can show that you understand these issues. Having a philosophical understanding will raise your awareness of how assumptions about the nature of knowledge impact on your thoughts and actions and enable you to remain conscious of the existence of alternative ways of thinking about knowledge. In turn, this will help you to defend your research from criticism, by showing that you made these choices knowingly, rather than unwittingly.

The philosophical ideas that inform a particular approach to knowledge creation are inextricably related to the methodologies and methods used to create it. Prasad (2005) argues that the notion of tradition captures the essential craft involved in developing and perfecting qualitative research skills and expertise which are passed on within communities. We very much like Prasad's definition and feel it is worth quoting at some length. She says a research tradition

> ... is best conceptualized as a complex ensemble of assumptions, worldviews, orientations, procedures and practices. A scholarly or

intellectual tradition intimates an entire *way of conducting scholar-ship* rather than merely offering a choice of technique or a uniform set of assumptions. (Prasad, 2005: 8, emphasis in original)

A related point has been made by Cunliffe (2011) who argues that management research should not just be judged on its scientific rigour, but instead ought to be seen as a craft, the pursuit of which results in something elegant, poetic or even beautiful.

Others have also argued that research is a form of craft, partly because of the high degree of uncertainty involved in its organisation (Whitley, 1984). This chimes with the views of sociologist C. Wright Mills (1959) who said that craftsmanship lies at the centre of social science research and also with the views of Denzin and Lincoln (2005) who argue that the qualitative researcher is a *bricoleur*, a kind of creative artist who makes things out of whatever happens to be available by piecing them together. Like Tony Becher in the quote at the start of this chapter, they also think that doing research is rather like making a patchwork quilt because it involves piecing together different methodo-logical tools and techniques to make a whole.

Another observation worth making at this point is that epistemo-logical issues are often closely bound up with your identity and in particular your prior educational experience. If you did an undergradu-ate degree in psychology where you were taught by a close group of positivist behavioural researchers and then you went on to do a masters degree where you came into contact with a diverse interdisciplinary group of social science researchers who shared an interest in critical research, you might understandably feel somewhat unsure as to which version of scientific knowledge is right. It takes quite a long time and significant effort to acquire, as well as to shed, a particular epistemo-logical stance. It can also be disturbing, because one way of thinking necessarily calls into question other ways and causes you to doubt their value and purpose. As a consequence, some researchers can become conflicted, switching between different philosophical positions in their research in a way which seems contradictory. For these reasons it can be quite revealing to know the educational background of a manage-ment researcher, including the discipline they originally trained in, since management researchers rarely leave their disciplinary hats at the door when they enter the business school. If you have a research supervisor, why not ask them.

We can only give the most cursory overview of various epistemologies and methodologies and point you in the direction of more detailed, substantive explanations in this short book. A great deal of ink has been spilled by philosophers, other social scientists, and management researchers, in their efforts to grapple with these complex and irresolvable intellectual problems. This chapter can only provide a very short introduction to them.

A troubling metaphor?

First, we will make what some readers might feel is a controversial analogy between management research and religion. Religion is a highly value laden and emotionally charged subject which people in many cultures are cautious about discussing. Added to this, many scientific researchers see their work as fundamentally located in the secular sphere, partly as a consequence of the Enlightenment, a cultural movement which began in England and France in the seventeenth century which transformed Western understandings of knowledge through the belief that it was possible to derive unambiguous truths about the world by applying objective, scientific methods of observation and reason. Even though some management researchers, such as postmodernists, reject this modernist worldview, they typically retain a suspicion of religion as associated with an era when knowledge was based on mysticism and superstition. We therefore need to make clear how and why we are drawing this analogy.

Religion, and in particular the idea of religious evolution referred to as the church-sect typology, which originated from the work of theologian Ernst Troeltsch (1912), offers an interesting way of thinking about the various philosophical traditions that exist within management research. The religious metaphor is revealing of aspects of management research that otherwise remain opaque, such as how followers of a particular philosophical tradition see themselves in relation to others. The metaphor of religion can help us to understand these patterns of behaviour. Using this metaphor also draws attention to the problem of circularity in philosophical traditions (Johnson and Duberley, 2000). In other words, attempts to judge the validity and contribution of each system of thought are grounded in the underlying assumptions each tradition makes about what counts as legitimate knowledge. They are thus self-referential and self-justifying (Morgan, 1983), unable to be evaluated objectively and independently of the epistemological assumptions that the researcher holds.

You might also have noticed that religious words, such as guru, orthodoxy and disciples, are sometimes used to talk about management research – we have already used some of them earlier in this book.

Becher (1989), who uses the metaphor of culture to understand academic research communities, describes the idols and artefacts that researchers use to indicate they belong to a particular 'tribe': 'the pictures on the walls and dust jackets of books kept in view are of ... Max Weber and Karl Marx and Emile Durkheim in the office of the sociologist' (Becher, 1989, citing Clark, 1980). Clearly the purpose of such ritual practices is to indicate reverence towards someone or something that stands apart from the mundane and the everyday, a distinctly religious characteristic. Similarly, Burrell and Morgan (1979) describe sociological thought as 'characterised by a narrow sectarianism' (1979: 22), a term that also has distinctly religious roots.

Paradigms and beliefs

Many well established ways of thinking about how research knowledge is created, and research communities formed, contain elements that complement the religious metaphor. Take for example Kuhn's (1970) notion of paradigms, widely used as a way of thinking about epistemological issues in management and other research disciplines. Kuhn suggested scientific knowledge is based on a set of universally shared *beliefs, values, ideas and techniques* that determine what researchers study, how they study it and how research findings are interpreted. During periods of paradigm stability, researchers work routinely, collectively and incrementally towards solving agreed upon puzzles and intellectual problems, a condition referred to as 'normal science'. During these periods, scientific knowledge is like a pile of sand, each new study a single grain added to it. Kuhn suggested a given paradigm exists within a scientific discipline until such a time when a growing number of anomalies present a challenge to it. While older, more established researchers remain committed to the old paradigm, newer, younger researchers with less to lose, seek to overthrow it. This provokes a crisis or paradigm shift, a revolution through which the old paradigm is overturned and a new one takes its place. For Kuhn, knowledge creation is a highly politicised process characterised by upheaval and power struggles. Interestingly, Kuhn thought that individual scientists experienced the change of allegiance from one paradigm to another as a conversion experience, akin to a change of religious faith, because no entirely rational explanation could be sufficient to justify the new paradigm over the old one.

In a landmark book which sought to map the field of organisational analysis, Burrell and Morgan (1979) argued that there was no single paradigm in management research. Instead, they said it could be classified into four different paradigms which they located within a two-by-two matrix. Along one axis the paradigms were labelled according to whether they were *objective*, treated 'the social world as if it were a hard, external, objective reality' (Burrell and Morgan, 1979: 3) or *subjective*, emphasising the importance of interaction and experience in constructing meaning in the social world. We prefer the term 'interpretive', as it is less evaluative than the label 'subjective', which is sometimes used pejoratively to mean not impartial or overly personal. Along the other axis, the paradigms were categorised as either *regulatory*, being concerned with describing what goes on in organisations, possibly suggesting minor changes that might lead to improvement but not making any fundamental judgements about whether what happens is right or wrong; or *radical*, making judgements about how organisations ought to be and suggesting how this could be achieved. They labelled the four paradigms radical humanism, radical structuralism, interpretive sociology and functionalist sociology.[1]

Note the use of the word *belief* in relation to the concept of paradigms. That is to say, they rely on prior assumptions about the nature of the world and how researchers ought to engage with it that cannot themselves be scientifically tested. As Burrell and Morgan's classification highlights, there is a moral aspect to paradigms, since they contain prescriptions about what ideas are good and worthwhile. In fact some people think that science is rather like a religion (Curry, 2006). According to such a view, the performance of scientific conventions like conducting experiments or carrying out regression analyses could be seen as religious rituals, a means of maintaining the belief that progress is based on scientific advances.

Positivism

Positivism is the dominant paradigm in management research. The origins of positivism are associated with the Enlightenment and the work of sociologist Auguste Comte in the early nineteenth century, who believed that knowledge must be based exclusively on what may be posited through direct, observational experience and that this applied to the social as well as the natural sciences. Comte's ideas were built upon by a group of intellectuals known as the Vienna Circle, who developed the central tenets of logical positivism, including the 'verification principle', which dictates that statements are 'senseless' unless they are capable of being verified empirically by gathering 'sense-data', which is factual knowledge derived through observation of an objective reality. Such knowledge is thought to be value free and objective and the researcher a neutral agent who, by holding a mirror up to the social world, can gain an accurate reflection of it. Positivism also operates according to a dualist ontology: it assumes that the research subject (for example, the organisational environment) and the object of study (e.g. the organisation itself) are separate, independent entities (Sandberg, 2005).

The aim of positivist researchers is to generate causal explanations and law-like statements about human social behaviour in managerial contexts. Positivist research is generally associated with quantitative methods because the collection and analysis of numerical data is seen as providing a more rigorous basis for generating objective knowledge (Daft, 1980). One of the striking things about positivist researchers is that they rarely discuss their assumptions in publication, 'reflecting, perhaps, that the dominance of this perspective is such that it is ingrained into common-sense assumptions about how to do research' (Johnson and Duberley, 2000: 38). A few writers have made statements vigorously defending and upholding the positivist tradition in management research and North American journals like *Organizational Research Methods* provide a forum in which discussions about the use of quantitative statistical techniques such as multivariate and factor analysis dominate. Donaldson (2008) in the memorably subtitled article, 'How I became a committed functionalist and positivist', reflects on his career as a management researcher. In an interesting aside he explains that his view of research was shaped by cultural and religious forces, including his education in Protestant schools where students were taught the value of saying what 'we believed to be the truth, even if it contradicted others or went against the norm or led us to suffer' (2008: 1073). His definition of positivism in management research is worth quoting at length.

> My view of organizations is positivist in several senses. It is a general theory of organizations, which holds across many different kinds of organizations and in many different settings ... The methods used to test the theory include scientific methods such as quantification and controlling for extraneous causes ... causal processes are conceived of as operating deterministically, with many of them involving objective forces that place pressures on the organization. It is also positivist in that material factors play

a role, e.g. organizational size, being the number of organizational members. (Donaldson, 2008: 1072)

Pfeffer (1993) argues that the development of what he calls 'organisational science' depends on greater paradigm consensus. The question of which paradigm should be favoured is not something he makes explicit, although his epistemological stance is consistently implied throughout the piece through the use of terms like 'scientific advancement' and his assertion that 'consensually shared beliefs about the nature of knowledge and methods in a field' enhances 'the ease and certainty of evaluating scientific research' (Pfeffer, 1993: 603). The alternative, he suggests, is for decisions relating to research quality to be based on 'particularistic criteria', such as the institutional affiliation of the author. Consequently, doctoral students struggle to distinguish 'good from bad theory and methods' (Pfeffer, 1993: 612). The implications of this are clear: the positivistic science model adopted by the natural sciences enables paradigm development, and paradigmatic plurality constitutes a threat to the development of the field.

Locating the positivist tradition of management research within our metaphorical framework of the church-sect continuum, it is distinctly church-like in character. Churches are the most established and powerful of religious institutions, claiming universality, exercising monopoly and seeking to eliminate competition. They recruit new members through reproduction and socialisation of children (aka new researchers) and have a bureaucratic, hierarchical structure. This enables appreciation of the activity that goes into establishing and maintaining positivism's strongly institutionalised position.

The institutionalised importance of positivism is illustrated by Grey's (2010) analysis of journal publishing patterns in organisation studies. The journals fall into two quite separate camps, one US and the other European. Prestigious US journals like *Administrative Science Quarterly* are heavily dominated by a positivist/functionalist orthodoxy which is self-referential and self-fulfilling. The logic works like this: explorations beyond the positivist paradigm are unlikely to get you published in the 'best' journals, where the 'best' and most highly cited authors publish, therefore positivist research is the 'right kind' of work (Grey, 2010: 683). But the global political landscape of management research has changed to such an extent that, for researchers in many business schools, only one camp is recognised, and that is the one defined by prestigious US journals.

Postpositivist responses

Use of the label postpositivist (the prefix denoting something that comes after), encompasses a broad range of beliefs, values, ideas and techniques that offer alternatives to positivism. The term is associated with Lincoln and Guba's (1985) book *Naturalistic Inquiry* and is used by Prasad (2005). We could have used the label 'anti-positivist' (Burrell and Morgan, 1979), although this doesn't so much tell you what it is, as what it's not, like anti-establishment or antibacterial. Postpositivist traditions are very diverse. Some, like Pfeffer (1993), see this as a weakness, whereas others, like Van Maanen (1995), see it as a source of strength and an alternative to the 'technocratic unimaginativeness' of management research with 'its inexplicable readiness to reduce the field to a set of unexamined, turgid, hypothetical thrusts' (Van Maanen, 1995: 139).

Looking at this through the lens of our metaphor, denominations are characterised by pluralism. A denomination arises when the church loses its position of complete dominance. Members of a denomination are permitted to have greater or lesser commitment and involvement and a degree of diversity around doctrine and practice is often tolerated. Postpositivist traditions of management research have grown in significance over the past 30 years, mainly through the efforts of researchers who have enhanced the legitimacy of these traditions through their research and community building activities. Qualitative research methods that focus on words and actions rather than numbers provide the building blocks of postpositivist research. The recent establishment of management journals dedicated to publishing such research, like *Qualitative Research in Organizations and Management* and *Journal of Organizational Ethnography*, represent attempts to carve out more space for postpositivist management research, even if much of this activity remains concentrated in European rather than US contexts. Within the postpositivist tradition there are two main groupings – interpretive researchers and post-structuralist researchers – which are discussed next.

Back to interpretivism

We could have chosen to refer to this philosophical tradition under the label social constructionism, which is sometimes used instead to describe research predicated on the belief that people shape their understandings of the world by interacting with one another. Some people use the label social constructivism to describe a similar research orientation. The main difference between the constructionists and the constructivists is that the -nists, including people like Kenneth Gergen (1999), are more concerned with collective meaning-making when people interact with one another whereas the -vists are more psychologically oriented, concentrating on individual processes of interpretation and cognition and how they are influenced by social processes. Here we have decided to stick with the label interpretivism but you should be aware that other people use terms like social constructionism to refer to broadly the same thing.

For the interpretive researcher, management can only be understood from the point of view of the people who are directly involved in it, including those who do various kinds of managing and those who are managed. This fundamental principle is derived from German sociologist Max Weber's theory of knowledge in the social sciences. Weber developed these ideas at the beginning of the twentieth century, prompted by an intellectual clash between natural scientists and social scientists on whether the latter could be considered to be using scientific methods to produce legitimate knowledge, a phenomenon known as the 'Methodenstreit' (Burger, 1987). Weber sought to distinguish between the methods of the natural and social sciences, to enable the knowledge claims of the latter to be considered legitimate. He argued that the demonstration of law-like regularities was not possible in the social sciences. He also claimed that facts never speak for themselves, instead they must be interpreted. Therefore, no science, social or otherwise, can be fundamentally neutral, either in its methods or the language used to describe the subject being studied. Weber's ideas were based on the notion that the study of human social action was fundamentally different from the objects and events studied by natural scientists because people are guided by values. The task of social science is to study how people understand their world, a concept he labeled *verstehen*, and saw as the basis of human conduct. The focus is on understanding the everyday lifeworlds that individuals inhabit, which they use to make sense of phenomena and construct a meaningful reality. This can lead to a participant observational fieldwork strategy based on 'letting the data speak', in which the researcher assumes that 'the explanation of particular events is already known collectively and severally by those who experience them and/or indeed have made them happen' (Lupton, 1985: 15). This is an insightful summation of what interpretivists see as the difference between studying physical and social phenomena. In the case of the latter, the social scientist is 'discovering' what her research participants already know. The goal of such research is 'thick description', a term that encapsulates the intellectual effort of interpreting the underlying meaning of behaviour as it is constructed by organisational members.

We can only briefly discuss a few of the methodologies associated with interpretivism in management research here. Those we focus on are ethnomethodology, dramaturgy and ethnography. Ethnomethodology is founded on the work of Harold Garfinkel (1967) and concerned with how people *accomplish* their everyday life through *routine action*. The methods used to explore social reality are based on very detailed analysis of naturally occurring linguistic and embodied behaviour, often using conversation analysis, a fine-grained method of analysing speech and action through which members produce accounts or sensemaking narratives. Conversation analysis takes account of even the slightest of utterances, pauses and interruptions (transcription protocols rely on a complex set of notational symbols), and emphasis is placed on analysing in detail a small number of relatively short interactional episodes, each perhaps lasting only a couple of minutes. In a recent book, Llewellyn and Hindmarsh (2010) provide a number of examples of management research that make use of this approach, often involving video as well as audio recorded methods of data collection. Yet they acknowledge that newcomers to the approach can be daunted by the 'seemingly masochistic level of detail at which organisational conduct is transcribed and analysed' (Llewellyn and Hindmarsh, 2010: 45). Ethnomethodologists believe that socially occurring phenomena are able to be discovered, rather than imagined. They thus adopt a relatively realist view of the world as having an external reality that exists independently of our attempts to understand it, which is somewhat divergent from other followers of the interpretive tradition.

Dramaturgy relies on the metaphor of the stage to suggest that social actors are engaged in trying to give a convincing performance in situations of face-to-face interaction. This provides a way of analysing the micro-level practices whereby individuals engage in frontstage efforts to give convincing presentations, and conceal other aspects of their identity, including those that may cause them to be stigmatised, in the backstage of their social life. Limited guidance is provided on methods of data collection that should be used, and Goffman (1959), whose work provides the foundations of the dramaturgical perspective, rarely demonstrated that he had collected data systematically and scientifically in the manner that we expect of researchers today. But this hasn't stopped the approach being adopted by management researchers, and today there is renewed interest in it as a way of going beyond language and focusing on the everyday action entailed in managerial work. Among other things, dramaturgy has been used to understand processes of managerial impression management, power and performance, and consultancy work.

Ethnography offers an alternative interpretive approach to generating knowledge about management. Some would see it as primarily a set of data-gathering techniques based on spending long periods engaged in participant observation in a fieldwork setting, and therefore more of a method than a methodology. However, we agree with writers like Agar (1980) and Wolcott (1999), who argue that ethnography offers a distinctive way of conceptualising, or seeing, as well as looking at, the social world by focusing on the patterns of shared behaviour that we label culture. The ethnographic study of organisations enjoyed a period of relative popularity during the 1990s due to the popularity of the concept of culture, marked by the publication of several book length studies of single organisations, such as those by Kunda (1992) and Watson (1994). More recently ethnography has become something of a niche territory. This is in no small part due to the challenges involved in doing ethnography, including the time-consuming and unpredictable nature of fieldwork. Once completed there are also challenges in publishing ethnographic research in a context where the performance of management researchers is measured by the number of journal articles they publish, since ethnographers often prefer to write up their research in the form of a book because they believe this is the best way of doing 'thick description', as the basis of understanding. Yet there are tentative signs of a resurgent interest in organisational ethnography in the form of special issues of journals (Cunliffe, 2010) and recent books on the subject (Neyland, 2008; Ybema et al., 2009).

More posts and a few turns

We are not yet finished in our exploration of 'posts' in this chapter, as postpositivism also encompasses a range of traditions associated with postmodernism. Postmodernism can be seen as a reaction against modernism, with its attendant beliefs in reason and observation as the basis for fundamental truth claims. When talking about postmodernism there is much talk of the 'turns' through which the direction of knowledge creation has been challenged, reversed or redirected. Used somewhat interchangeably, the concepts of the *linguistic* and *postmodern* turn stem from the critique of the Enlightenment and its portrayal of scientific study as the basis of human progress. Just to confuse matters further this is sometimes called the cultural turn, not to be confused with the narrative or textual turn, which we will return to shortly. The linguistic turn is associated with postmodern philosophers like Rorty

(1979), who suggests scientific study is essentially a culturally specific *language-game* played by members of academic communities in order to persuade one another of the truthfulness of their claims. They assert that knowledge is essentially undiscoverable and continually open to revision. Even natural scientists are suggested to promote legitimating *metanarratives*, convenient fictions that provide a basis for knowledge and action. The implication of this is to call into question realist/ objectivist assumptions about a material world that can be studied and instead to argue that that the entity we know of as management cannot exist independently of the linguistic terminology and symbolic structures used to represent it.

Related to postmodernism is the notion of poststructuralism, which is closely aligned with the work of Foucault (1977) and Derrida (1976). Poststructuralism is also concerned with language, conceptualised as a set of ideas and implicit rules about how one should behave. Such discourses shape an individual's self identity and discipline them into particular social relationships and forms of action, thereby constituting the basis of power in society. Derrida (1976) argued that linguistic meaning was relational, based on hierarchical relationships where the superior meaning of one term was derived from the inferior meaning of its opposite. Other poststructuralists like Barthes (1967) drew attention to the dynamic nature of linguistic meaning making, as open to continual contestation, often independently of the author who uttered or wrote the words in the first place.

Hence the task for postmodern and poststructuralist management researchers is one of *deconstruction*, to reveal and question the representational processes used to represent management. Postmodernism and poststructuralism have exerted a profound influence on management studies over the past 25 years and have promoted a fascination with language as the basis of meaning-making in organisational life. Here we introduce three linguistically focused research methodologies that have attracted particularly strong followings, namely semiotic, discourse and narrative analysis.

Semiotic analysis is concerned with what its followers call the duality of the sign, which is the relationship between the *signifier*, most commonly a word, and the *signified*, the thing that the word represents. Structuralist semioticians, whose work is informed by the linguistic philosopher Saussure (1916), see the meaning of signs as relatively unproblematic, together forming an entire system of meaning, most obviously in the form of an entire language. Philosophers like Barthes and Derrida later provided the foundations for a poststructuralist, critical or social semiotic tradition, in which signs are seen as *polysemic*, influenced by the social context where they are used in a way which enables the privileging of certain interpretations, or *readings*, over others. This potentially gives rise to a much more critical, fluid analysis of semiotic meaning-making in organisations that engages with all kinds of *texts*, including visual images as well as words, which are often overlooked by management researchers.

Discourse analysis, which is fundamentally concerned with the written and spoken word, has gathered a tremendous following in management research over the past ten years or so, as illustrated by the number of handbooks, journal articles and conferences dedicated to promoting it. Key social scientific influences come from the work of Potter and Wetherell (1987) and Fairclough (1995). A good place to start is with the work of Hardy (2001), who could be seen as a high priestess of organisational discourse analysis. While all discourse analysis is postpositivistic, some management researchers in this tradition are more interpretive, while others are more poststructuralist or critical in orientation.

Lastly in our discussion of 'posts' and turns, we must mention narrative and storytelling research. Like discourse analysis, this way of studying management now attracts a sizable and loyal following, with regular conferences and research seminars dedicated to understanding narratives and storytelling in organisations. The focus is on identifying what counts as a story, through notions such as plot and characterisation, and on analysing how they are performed and challenged. High priests and priestesses in this area include Czarniawska (1998), Gabriel (2000) and Boje (1991, 2001), each of whom has published widely on this subject. As with discourse analysis, followers may be more or less critical (poststructuralist or structuralist) in orientation.

Protest and change in philosophies of management research

Returning once again to our metaphor, we reach the protest end of the church-sect continuum. Sect members often see themselves as the embodiment of true believers, advocating a return to original religious teaching which they see other groups as having strayed away from. Because this is an evolutionary continuum, some sects move towards denominational status as they grow in size, while others do not survive. A third possibility is that sects retain elements of radical protest and commitment to ideology while avoiding becoming a denomination. This is achieved as a consequence of becoming relatively self-sufficient from wider society. As an example, we briefly introduce the tradition of critical realism, which advocates that postmodernists and poststructuralists have strayed too far in their view of reality as socially constructed. This is not because we want to single out critical realism; there are several other management research philosophies that we could have chosen, but it provides a useful example.

Critical realism involves yet another turn,[2] this time the *realist turn* which challenges the linguistic turn for its apparent 'descent into discourse' (Harvey, 1996: 85, cited in Reed, 2005: 1626). These ideas were originally developed by the philosopher Bhaskar (1978) and translated into a methodological framework for social scientists by the sociologist Archer (1995). Critical realism focuses on the material effects of what they describe as *deep*, *underlying* social structures, or *generative mechanisms*, which they believe 'exist and act independently of the patterns and events they generate' at a surface level and can be studied through empirical analysis (Reed, 2005: 1625). The realism in critical realism is different from the scientific or naive realism associated with positivism, in which it is believed that knowledge can be gained purely empirically through gathering sense data. Critical realists call for management studies to return to focusing on the socio-material forces of economy and power relations which they believe have been collapsed into notions of discourse, culture and identity.

One of the strengths of critical realism is suggested to reside in its ability to overcome the structure/agency problem in management research, which is a longstanding social scientific dilemma about the extent to which human beings can shape their social world, even though their ability to do so is constrained by the structural conditions in which their actions are located. This is also referred to as the dialectic of control in human action (Giddens, 1984). Giddens argued that the prioritisation of either micro or macro phenomena is a 'phoney war' because both are reliant on one other. Another strength of critical realism relates to its potential in transcending the binary opposition between positivist and postpositivistic paradigms. Neither positivist nor constructionist critical realists argue that it is a mistake to begin with epistemological assertions. Critical realists recognise that there are likely to be certain stabilities in the environment and there is likely to be something behind them (referred to as event regularities). These will not necessarily always occur in the same shape or form and whatever it is that produces these events can't always be relied on. It is also recognised that these events will vary, depending on situation and context, and that understanding of these contexts and situations is seen as extremely important. Critical realists see the world as an open system with emergent properties – rather than a closed and deterministic system with stable properties (as positivists would like us to believe is the case), or even (as constructionists might suggest), where there is no reality other than the meaning we place on it (an extreme constructionist view). A number of management researchers have been attracted to critical realism over the past decade, particularly those who are interested in how managerial structures under capitalism are used to exploit and oppress workers.

The flourishing of cults

Similar to sects, cults are distinguishable primarily through being concerned with discovering new or rediscovering forgotten aspects of a religion. Typically small, informal and relatively transitory and short-lived, cults are often centred on charismatic leaders who play an important role in advocating the cult's particular doctrinal position. There are a number of emergent philosophies of management research which we might think of in these terms.

Cult-like flourishing is both a potential strength and a weakness. On the plus side, there is a great deal to choose from in this philosophical marketplace. Getting on board with a currently fashionable philosophy of knowledge can be quite exciting and can help you to get your work published by enabling you to join a community of practice and giving you access to a ready-made audience for your research findings. On the other hand, the criticisms that have been levelled at management fashions can also be applied to philosophies of management knowledge – namely that they are simply 'old wine in new bottles', ideas that have been repackaged but essentially remain the same. Hence the advice Eccles and Nohria (1992) give to managers is also relevant to management researchers. Understanding the way ideas are (re)used is more important than grasping every new buzzword that comes along as if it was the equivalent of the Holy Grail. Additionally, as has been noted in management practice, the relentless pursuit of fashion is exhausting and there is a danger that its continual pursuit results in transience and superficiality of understanding, rather like the difference between buying cheaply made clothes produced using sweatshop labour and throwing them away after one season, versus purchasing a few well made, classic garments that will last you a lifetime.

Here we focus on a recent philosophical grouping in management research which can be construed as an embrace of something lost or forgotten in the knowledge creation process, namely the study of management as a process and a practice. We treat these two trends as overlapping, but enthusiastic debates have been waged between the proponents of each as to whether they constitute separate or interrelated philosophical perspectives and what, if anything, differentiates them. Processual perspectives are often denoted, following Weick (1969), by the use of verbs such as 'becoming'. In organisation studies the focus is on organising, in strategy research it is strategising, and so on. Social reality is seen as continually unfolding, temporally, contextually and holistically, the emphasis being placed on the flow of action. Like critical realists, practice researchers also seek to address the tension between studying micro-phenomena of interaction in everyday life, while simultaneously relating them to macro-phenomena, including the social institutions that shape them (Whittington, 2006). However, whether this represents a genuinely new epistemological stance, or is simply a re-articulation of existing philosophical principles which are already well established within the interpretive tradition, is debatable.

Conclusion

Philosophically speaking, you have to 'be something'. This is a piece of advice that we often hear being given to new management researchers. Finding a philosophical position you are comfortable with takes time and shapes not just your research findings, but also, as we will discuss in the next chapter, the questions that you think are worth asking. Your epistemological stance also forms part of your identity as a researcher, something that defines who you are and how others see you. Of course, it is possible to change your philosophical position but this will probably require a significant shift in self identity and your actions may be viewed with suspicion by other researchers, who may interpret this as a sign of inconsistency.

More commonly, management researchers find a philosophical position they are comfortable with and stick to it. Over the course of a research career, commitment to a particular philosophy of knowledge can encourage researchers to concentrate on methods of data collection and analysis that complement it. This is partly because they invest time and energy in becoming proficient in using and explaining certain methods. As a result, their 'interpretive repertoire' (the paradigmatic, theoretical and methodological understandings that they bring to bear on their research (Alvesson and Sköldberg, 2000)) tends to narrow, and their research becomes progressively more specific.

If the dominant tradition in management research is positivist, it might seem to make sense simply to join the church. Certainly you can't ignore it, and many researchers would agree that, at the very least, you need a rudimentary understanding of the main philosophical traditions in management research in order to make an informed decision about how to situate your own practice, and to counter criticism of your research from researchers following different traditions. But if you join a philosophical tradition simply because it is the biggest and strongest, perhaps because you think being part of it will make your research more accepted and your life easier, we can't help but feel that something is lost through this. In the UK, it has been observed that some people write 'Church of England' on forms which ask your religion, even though they don't attend church – except perhaps for weddings and funerals. Sociologists call this nominal religious affiliation, or belonging without believing. Of course, belonging is itself an important source of self identity but we think it is important for such choices to be made on the basis of values about what research is for and why we do it. Whatever temple it is that you worship, this should be done in good faith and with a degree of conviction towards the principles upon which the philosophy is founded.

Notes

1   The fact that Burrell and Morgan label two of their paradigms as 'sociology' gives an insight into the status of management research at the time the book was written as, prior to the 1960s, organisation theory was known as the sociology of organisations.
2   Contu and Willmott (2005) suggest that management researchers would be spinning if they followed all of these turns.

4

Methods of Management Research

> The choice and adequacy of a method embodies a variety of assumptions regarding the nature of knowledge and the methods through which that knowledge can be obtained, as well as a set of root assumptions about the nature of the phenomenon to be investigated. (Gareth Morgan and Linda Smircich, 1980: 491)

> The problem is not so much lack of variety in the practice of method, as in the hegemonic and dominatory pretensions of certain versions or accounts of method. (John Law, 2004: 4)

This chapter explores how management researchers choose what methods to use in their research and how the quality of these methods is assessed by others. These choices are complex, and involve practical, philosophical and political considerations. Although it is generally recognised as a crude oversimplification, management research is commonly divided into two camps, labelled quantitative and qualitative. Some management researchers position themselves exclusively on one side or other of the quantitative/qualitative methods divide. This decision is partly driven by a desire for paradigmatic consistency which, as we have said, involves having a set of beliefs about what constitutes knowledge and how to go about finding it. For example, interviewing is a qualitative method that is usually associated with an interpretive stance, whereas questionnaire surveys are quantitative methods generally used by positivist researchers. But as we shall see, just because you use one kind of method doesn't automatically mean you are adopting a particular philosophical position, because the way in which you use the method is shaped by the worldview to which you subscribe. The binary distinction between quantitative and qualitative methods is made problematic by this, as we will explain shortly.

Choices about what methods to use have a significant bearing on how your research will be regarded and who will read it. Certain management journals, for example, hardly publish any research that uses qualitative methods, and this inevitably, and rather sadly, has a bearing on new researchers' decisions about what methods to use. Some management researchers take a mixed methods approach, combining quantitative together with qualitative methods, in the same study. In this chapter we will review the recent trend towards mixed methods in management research and ask what makes this approach currently popular.

Despite the apparent high degree of choice, there is what institutional theorists would describe as a tendency towards mimetic isomorphism in the use of methods in management research. This involves emulating what other successful, high-profile researchers have done before, or citing key methodological sources, as a way of accruing legitimacy. Hence, some methods and methodological points of reference are used extensively, some might say excessively, while others, especially more innovative methods such as internet or visual research, take a long time to catch on and tend to be seen as somewhat risky.

In this chapter we will not explain how to use the various methods that can be used to collect and analyse data, as there are a great many other books and articles that explain how to do this. A more important reason for not focusing on methods relates to the article by Morgan and Smircich, quoted at the start of this chapter. They argue that the focus on methods in management research is problematic because it gives the 'illusion' that it is the methods *themselves* which generate particular forms of knowledge, and not the researcher. The tendency for particular kinds of method to be seen as ends in themselves, they suggest, results in abstracted empiricism (whether quantitative or qualitative), and can degenerate into a debate about the relative merits of quantitative versus qualitative methods. This focuses attention on epistemological issues of how to generate knowledge, rather than on what are perhaps more important ontological questions, such as: what is there to be known? In this chapter we will therefore keep our discussion of methods firmly connected to other aspects of research design and methodology, including the kinds of question posed, and the underlying assumptions about the nature of knowledge that this presumes. Once you have thought about these issues, you can then go off and learn about the particular research methods you are interested in.

We will also be arguing against a standardised approach to the use of methods in management research, sometimes characterised by the citation of certain key writers almost routinely in methodology sections of published articles, rather like a religious catechism, without the researcher necessarily engaging with the methodological source in a meaningful way at all, and often without acknowledging that there are alternative approaches. An example of this is Glaser and Strauss (1967) who are cited by management researchers at the merest mention of grounded theory, sometimes when there is not very good justification for doing so.

Method fits the question

One place to start in deciding what methods to use is with your research question. You might begin by reading and reviewing the literature to find out what is already known about the topic you are interested in and what aspects of it remain limitedly understood. If you are a positivist researcher you will be looking to develop a research question related to your topic that focuses on an independent variable, which you suspect may have a causal influence on the dependent variable or variables. Your question is likely to be concerned with 'how many' patterns, explored through the collection of numerical data. You may then translate these variables into a series of empirically testable hypotheses.

To take another example, if you are a discourse analyst, your analysis of the literature will concentrate on how your topic of interest is constructed discursively. It will be intoned by conceptual terms such as 'repertoires' and 'genres', which are associated with a discursive methodology. Your question will probably be concerned with understanding processes and how things work, such as 'how is this topic being constructed through the discourse?' and 'what are the functions and consequences of this?' You will need to collect qualitative, linguistic data to address this.

Having developed a question or series of hypotheses, you would then decide what methods to use to collect data to enable the question to be answered. For the positivist researcher this might involve administering a questionnaire survey to a statistically representative sample of the population that you are interested in finding out about. For the discourse analyst, methods would be chosen that enable the collection of data about various forms of talk. This might include contrived talk (such as from interviews carried out and transcribed by the researcher), or naturally occurring talk (for example based on the transcripts of formal meetings).

Once you have collected your data, you need to use systematic techniques to analyse it. For the positivist researcher this would typically entail quantitative analysis involving the application of statistical procedures, probably using a software tool such as SPSS or Minitab. Discourse analysis might involve the use of techniques for fine coding talk, including various textual protocols for recording interruptions, intonations and pauses in speech.

Both researchers would then look for interesting patterns in the data related to their research questions as the basis for relating back to existing theory. For the positivist researcher this would involve using the data to reject, prove or revise the hypotheses originally set. Findings may be presented using tables and diagrams which are discussed in order to draw conclusions. For the discursive researcher, sifting through the data would hopefully result in the emergence of a theory to explain the patterns observed. Presentation and interpretation of the data would focus on particularly illuminating extracts of speech which highlighted issues related to the research questions. In both cases tables, diagrams or extracts would be included in the final article, book or report, to explain the findings and demonstrate and give confidence in the conclusions drawn.

There are some who think that the choice between various research methods is akin to selecting 'the right tool for the job'. In other words, once you know what your research question is, you can identify the most suitable method to answer it. Choices about which methods to use are therefore dependent on the research question. The management researcher could metaphorically be seen as like a car mechanic, delving into their toolkit to find the instrument that enables a particular problem to be solved. But this portrayal is misleading because it implies that research design is a linear, sequential process where the researcher starts by finding a philosophical position, then develops a question, and only then chooses the methods they deem suitable to answer it. In our experience, the majority of management research doesn't work like this.

A messy business

One reason for this relates to the serendipitous nature of the research process which means that interesting empirical phenomena often arise opportunistically. Organisations are a constant feature of our lives. As Henry Mintzberg noted, most of us in the developed world are born in an organisation (usually as a hospital), we are educated and work in organisations all our lives and even when we die, organisations are involved. Consequently, much of the empirical material that management research focuses on is all around us all the time. This proximity to the subject of study means that potential research opportunities are ever present, even in an organisation that you work for. We have already given examples of how our organisational experience has shaped our research, and we doubt we are unusual in this. Research is thus driven by curiosity, which is shaped (and limited) by opportunity.

An example of this can be found in the area of strategy research, where a lot of qualitative empirical research has explored senior managerial work in universities. This is partly because gaining research access to the contexts where strategy works is notoriously difficult, due to the sensitivity of the practice and the power of the people involved. When studying organisations with which you are familiar the process of data collection is more likely to be emergent and spontaneous (Alvesson, 2003). This means that you wait for interesting things to pop up. In such situations the researcher does not have a clear research question in advance of the study and the imposition of a systematic analytical framework occurs after the opportunity to conduct research has been identified.

But these are not the only circumstances in which the question driven model doesn't correspond to research practice. For example, some management research is based on secondary data, such as involving analysis of official statistical or survey data produced by government agencies or international bodies, or documentary analysis of text and images in company annual reports. Researchers who use this type of data are severely limited in their choice of research question by what kind of data is contained in the secondary source. They are also constrained in their choice of methods that can be used to analyse it. Similarly, there are situations where data collected and partially analysed by one researcher, for example as part of a research degree, is subsequently analysed by another researcher, who brings their particular theoretical perspective to bear on the data retrospectively.

Another reason why the 'right method for the question' approach often doesn't work is because data doesn't automatically lead to the production of theory. In other words, data does not emerge independently of theory, but from the worldview used to inform the research questions. Research questions are thus shaped by the theoretical stance you have adopted. The extent to which a researcher's worldview frames the questions they ask and the knowledge generated is illustrated in a classic article by Hassard (1991). Hassard attempts to carry out 'multiple paradigm research', studying the same research setting, an emergency fire service organisation, using each of the four paradigms set out by Burrell and Morgan (1979). What is striking about this is the extent to which research questions and the methods used to answer them are shaped by the paradigm. The important point here is that research question and methods are mutually constituting, and both are shaped by the philosophical stance taken.

A related point is made by Alvesson and Kärreman (2007), who argue that the frameworks, pre-understandings and vocabularies associated with a particular theoretical position are crucial in constructing a particular view of the world using research data. They say it is the interaction between theoretical assumptions and empirical impressions that results in theory development. A particular feature of this process involves the occurrence of what they call 'breakdowns', when unexpected puzzles arise that cannot be explained using existing theory. This account emphasises the agency of the researcher in the analytical process, who is not simply mirroring the external world but actively shaping meaning in relation to it.

Theorising is thereby characterised as a process of 'disciplined imagination' based on dialogic reflection. Research methods that enable a degree of flexibility in responding to breakdowns are favoured by Alvesson and Kärreman as ways of developing interesting theory, rather than that which is obvious or absurd. But the most important thing is that theory is seen as framing data (Alvesson and Kärreman prefer the label 'empirical material', as a way of drawing attention to the plasticity of data), rather than the other way around.

To understand the importance of flexibility we must turn to one of the most influential pieces of management research ever carried out, known as the Hawthorne studies (Roethlisberger and Dickson, 1939). The scale of this research project was ambitious. It began in 1924 when the Western Electric Company's Industrial Research Division, with the aid of government funding, carried out a series of experiments to understand issues relating to worker job satisfaction, monotony and productivity. The findings from this initial phase of study were inconclusive, so in 1927 the company turned to researchers from Harvard Business School and asked them to come into the Chicago, Illinois based plant, to carry out more research. Initially, the Harvard researchers carried out further experiments, which involved creating controlled experimental conditions in the plant, where particular variables such as lighting levels and rest breaks were deliberately altered and the results measured, produced confusing and contradictory results. The researchers eventually concluded that this was the result of the study itself, as the very fact of being the focus of investigators' attention seemed to be causing worker productivity levels to rise, a finding that has come to be known as the 'Hawthorne effect' (Schwartzman, 1993). This led them to rethink the entire approach of the study, turning instead towards 'psychological factors' and using interviews to find out what workers said were the reasons for their behaviour, i.e. their *words*, supplemented by direct observations to find out what they actually did in a work context, i.e. their *actions*. The study was eventually discontinued by Western Electric in 1933, but not before the researchers had conducted countless experimental episodes, recorded findings from numerous 'behavioural observations' and interviewed more than 21,000 people (Roethlisberger and Dickson, 1939).

It is not simply the scale of the study which makes the Hawthorne research important. Nor does its significance derive primarily from the coining of the phrase, the 'Hawthorne effect', although this is significant in revealing the limitations associated with classical scientific methods such as experiments in the context of management research. What the study also shows is the importance of flexibility and adaptability in management research, as the researchers changed their research questions and subject focus quite radically after they were already involved in data collection, rather than continuing along the same experimental lines as before (Dickson and Roethlisberger, 1966, cited in Schwartzman, 1993). This ability to cope with uncertainty and take calculated risks are things that interpretive researchers are often more comfortable with, through seeing theory building and data collection as cyclical or iterative, and thus potentially requiring a change of direction as the research progresses. This is consistent with the arguments of Paul Feyerabend (1993), who says that theory development must allow for the proliferation of alternatives to the theory being tested, even if the 'facts' as currently known do not support it.

A final reason why the question-driven approach to methods choice fails to work is because not all kinds of research rely equally on the prior development of a clearly focused research question. For example, ethnographers commonly talk about 'grand tour' questions, which are used in interactions with research participants to facilitate detailed consideration of a cultural scene. Such exploratory questions might be along the lines of 'could you describe for me the kinds of things that you do?' or 'please tell me about your work'. Of course, these questions are just a starting point from which further questions evolve, but they highlight the difficulty in assuming that research proceeds in a linear fashion on the basis of a predetermined research question that is developed through engagement with a distinct literature that deals with a certain topic or subject. And it is not just interpretive research where such issues arise, for it can be the case in other kinds of research that questions are developed (or at least revised) retrospectively, in order to overcome the problem that the data collected does not answer the question that the researcher had hoped it would. This type of 'reverse engineering' portrays the research process as more linear and logical than if the researcher was to explain that the original research question turned out not to be very helpful, and therefore they changed it to one that the data could more reasonably address.

Measuring research quality

Choices about what research methods to use are made in the context of how this is likely to be judged. Whether you are interested in getting a good grade in your dissertation, hoping to gain a research award or looking to get your findings published, a set of criteria will be applied by those who evaluate your work as to whether it is of sufficient quality. For positivist researchers, judgements about the truthfulness of research as an accurate reflection of reality are based on assessment of *internal* and *external validity*, and *reliability*. Here is an example. Imagine you are researching how human resource management (HRM) practices are used in small businesses, and, if they are, what effects they have on business performance. Obviously you first need to define what you mean by 'human resource management practices'. From previous research you can put together a list of practices like performance appraisal, structured training opportunities, and so on. Then you need to build a working definition of organisational performance. Positivist management research often works according to the principle of operationalism, using observable indicators as proxies for the actual variables that they want to generalise about (Johnson and Duberley, 2000). To measure organisational performance, you will probably use financial measures as proxies, such as turnover or profit, which may be combined with other 'softer' measures such as employee turnover. These definitions form the basis for your questionnaire in which you ask questions to find out if managers are using HRM techniques and generate some data on organisational performance over time. Finally, after testing your questionnaire on a few willing friends (piloting, as the formal term goes), your respondents (managers in your sample of small companies) receive the questionnaire, by post or (more likely) online, and hopefully complete it for you. You've got your data. It is now time to input it and run those statistical tests that enable you to show whether or not HRM practices affect small business performance.

There are numerous threats to internal validity present here. The conclusion you reach relies on demonstrating an exclusive causal relationship between the independent variable (HRM practices) and the dependent variable (organisational performance), by ruling out alternative explanations, including the possibility that the direction of causality is the reverse of what you are suggesting. This relies on demonstrating that you did all you could to eliminate the possibility that other independent, or intervening variables, influenced your results. There are also threats to external validity, or whether your results can be generalised beyond the context where the data was collected. You therefore need to show that your sample – of managers in small companies – is representative of the population (all small businesses) that you wish to generate knowledge about. For instance, if the managers are all male and all work in engineering firms, how might this have affected your results and your ability to generalise from them? Lastly, in terms of reliability, if another researcher came along and tried to replicate or repeat your study, using a different group of managers, would they get the same results? And judgements of quality based on internal and external validity, and reliability are only the beginning. Other quality criteria can also include replicability, measurement validity, ecological validity, construct validity, convergent validity, face validity and predictive validity. One of the ways management researchers defend themselves in the light of these evaluations is by being very clear in their presentation of findings about the limitations of a study.

All these quality criteria are, to a greater or lesser extent, seen as less appropriate in evaluating postpositivist research. The crucial difference arises from the fact that in postpositivist paradigms there is no presumption of the existence of a single shared reality against which research findings can be compared. Meaning is therefore not presumed to have a universal quality. Hence it is not assumed that things will be understood in the same way by everyone. Therefore, judgements of research quality must be carefully contextualised, and are reliant on assessments of whether the research corresponds to the researcher's and research participants' understandings of reality may be evaluated using criteria like respondent validation, which involves sharing research findings with research participants to see if they agree with them. This helps to establish the 'communicative validity' of the study, based on whether a community of researchers and research participants are able to develop a shared understanding of what is going on in a situation (Sandberg, 2005). Key to notions of truth within the interpretive tradition is the notion that they rely on the researcher's understanding of the research object. Truth is thus contingent or unfinished. It is also perspectival in the sense that it is actively constituted using different analytic methodologies (such as narrative analysis versus discourse analysis), which result in different aspects of the phenomenon being emphasised.

Positivist anxiety

And yet the criteria most commonly used to assess management research quality are shaped by positivist norms of scientific practice. As we have already said, criteria such as validity and reliability are based on the assertion of notions of an objective reality and truth. As a consequence of the dominance of these norms and values in determining what constitutes research quality, qualitative management researchers tend to be affected by positivist anxiety, 'manifested as an eagerness to measure up to conventional positivist standards' (Prasad, 2005: 4). This causes them to apply criteria for evaluating quantitative research, even if this is inconsistent with their paradigmatic position, for example by talking about the avoidance of bias. Positivist anxiety is exacerbated by concerns about the lack of a 'boilerplate' (Pratt, 2009), in the form of universal quality standards that can be applied to all qualitative research. Indeed a substantial amount of qualitative research in the field 'can be described as constituting a form of qualitative positivism' (Prasad and Prasad, 2002: 6) which uses nonquantitative (or nonstatistical) methods of data collection and analysis but makes traditional positivistic assumptions about the nature of social and organisational reality and the production of knowledge. Ontologically speaking, reality is therefore assumed to be concrete and separate from the researcher and knowledge is seen as able to be generated through the application of 'so-called objective methods' (Prasad and Prasad, 2002: 6). The global prevalence of these views cannot be underestimated. When Emma visited India and the Middle East recently, she found these neopositivist assumptions were particularly prevalent, and it was not uncommon for management researchers to declare emphatically that alternatives to positivism were simply not valid research.

This tendency is particularly evident in case study research, which relies mainly on qualitative methods such as interviews, observations and documentary analysis, in addition to quantitative methods like questionnaire surveys. One of the most highly cited articles about case study-based management research is by Eisenhardt (1989), which clocks up literally thousands of citations on Google Scholar. Eisenhardt offers what she describes as a 'roadmap' for doing inductive case study research to build theory. Her key points of reference are writers like Yin (1984), another widely cited case study methodologist, and Glaser and Strauss (1967), the progenitors of grounded theory. Eisenhardt 'extends' this work by advocating 'a priori specification of constructs' which can be 'explicitly' and more accurately 'measured' during the data collection, providing a 'firmer empirical grounding' for the study (Eisenhardt, 1989: 536). Although she acknowledges the possibility of 'serendipitous findings', these are seen as an extreme rarity.

Selection of cases is recommended based on theoretical sampling, but oddly this is focused on identifying the overall population from which the sample is drawn, a principle more oriented towards ensuring statistical representativeness rather than theoretical saturation. She also recommends that researchers work in teams, assigning the role of distanced observer to certain members to ensure objectivity. Finally, Eisenhardt makes a series of recommendations concerning data analysis, advocating the presentation of data in tabulated form to deal with the problem of 'data asphyxiation' and establish generalisability through pattern recognition based on cross-case comparison. Eisenhardt's desired end result is 'hypothesis shaping', based on 'measuring constructs and verifying the relationship between them' (Eisenhardt, 1989: 543), which in turn enables the development of testable propositions. Throughout, the language used reflects evaluative measures such as generalisability and internal validity, that are associated with quantitative research, rather than reflecting the concerns more usually associated with qualitative research, such as seeing through the eyes of the people studied. At no point does Eisenhardt propose any alternative to the traditional quantitative measures of quality, such as credibility or authenticity, which some would see as much more appropriate ways of assessing the quality of qualitative research.

This ethos is shared by Miles and Huberman (1994), whose 'sourcebook', first published in the mid 1980s, provides a set of codified procedures for reducing and displaying (using matrices, graphs, charts and networks) in order to 'verify' qualitative data. This book has proved popular in management research. Its rationale reveals much about positivist anxiety and the reasons for its existence when one of the authors writes:

> the most serious and central difficulty in the use of qualitative data is that the methods of analysis are not well formulated. For quantitative data, there are clear conventions the researcher can use. But the analyst faced with a bank of qualitative data has very few guidelines for protection against self-delusion, let alone the presentation of unreliable or invalid conclusions to scientific or policy-making audiences. How can we be sure that an 'earthy', 'undeniable' or 'serendipitous' finding is not, in fact *wrong*. (Miles, 1979: 591, emphasis in original)

What is most interesting about this approach is its antipathy towards words, or what Miles and Huberman call 'extended text', which they see as bulky and cumbersome and likely to overload our information-processing capabilities. Through their attempts to make qualitative data display more systematic and demonstrably truthful, Miles and Huberman's approach to qualitative analysis seems oriented towards convincing positivists that qualitative research methods are as precise and accurate as quantitative methods, through conforming to similar quality criteria and analytic conventions.

Ten years later, in the second edition of their book, Miles and Huberman added an extended section on the use of qualitative analysis software packages like Atlas.ti and NVivo. Some researchers have argued that the use of software in qualitative analysis is indicative of attempts to clean up the messiness of qualitative research and make its knowledge claims more acceptable to the scientific community and research gatekeepers. Computerised qualitative analysis represents a metaphor for systematicity, objectivity and rigour (Kelle, 1997), and has been suggested to have encouraged a form of technological determinism or methodological anomie (Richards and Richards, 1998), wherein research questions are designed to fit software programmes, which for example, implicitly favour grounded theory, further eroding methodological diversity.

This approach overlays a series of traditional positivistic assumptions about the nature of knowledge and how to go about building it, onto interpretive research. Its impact on qualitative management research is very evident, especially the emphasis on theory building based on *a priori* construct definition. Hence it is not enough to tell a convincing story through the data based on existing theory, instead qualitative researchers (particularly those who want to publish in elite journals) engage in inductive theory-building which lays the foundations for deductive testing using quantitative methods. Published articles of this kind often build complex process flow models on the basis of the research findings. These conventions within qualitative management research have become so prevalent that in seeking legitimacy, qualitative researchers are increasingly mimicking deductive, quantitative studies, through such things as forming propositional statements that are stylistically similar to hypotheses and performing statistical inter-rater reliability checks in order to conform to an 'intellectual milieu dominated by positivism' (Cornelissen et al., 2012: 199).

The pursuit of generalisability

Rather than measuring all management research according to positivist quality standards, perhaps we should look more closely at whether these standards actually measure things that are meaningful and useful. Take the classic example of the Aston studies, an ambitious programme of organisational research carried out in Birmingham, England in the 1960s. The purpose of the Aston studies was to enable systematic comparison across different types of organisation which in turn would enhance the potential for generalisation. Pugh and his colleagues wanted to find out what problems were specific to certain kinds of organisations and which problems were common to all types of organisation. The studies spanned multiple levels of analysis, including organisational structure, group dynamics, individual personality and behaviour, and the interactions between them. They started by using quantitative survey methods to look at issues such as technology, organisational size and markets and this formed the basis for more detailed case study analysis.

The researchers studied over 50 manufacturing and service firms in a diverse range of sectors. They later replicated the design of the original project in a range of other types of organisation. The Aston researchers wanted to be able to generalise and predict how various structural (such as the degree of centralisation) and contextual (for example the company's ownership and history) issues would affect organisational performance and behaviour.

What did they find? The disappointing answer is surprisingly little, mostly related to organisational structure rather than group or individual behaviour. Pugh's summary of the Aston studies findings is insightful in this regard. He states that the main achievements were to develop 'a useful heuristic framework of stable, meaningful variables applied to organisational functioning and behaviour', adding that this 'is important if we are to develop through a descriptive to an analytical discipline' (Pugh, 1981: 160). But the precise impact of the relationships between all of the variables studied is much more difficult to discern. This, argues Starbuck (1981), is not the fault of the researchers, who upheld the highest standards of research methodology, but a consequence of the overambitious nature of their intentions, which were to establish general propositions about organisations of different kinds. This is not to say that the findings were uninteresting, but that the researchers were unrealistic in their initial goals. Starbuck likens this to trying to study the relations between structure and technology across animals, including whether they live in herds or hives, and the nature of their specialised roles – laying eggs, hunting, etc. The point is that although general correlations might be established, they would probably be very uninformative. Generalisability might therefore not be worth pursuing so enthusiastically.

Statistical (in)significance

In a book called *The Cult of Statistical Significance,* historical economists Ziliak and McCloskey (2008) argue that statistical significance, the main scientific tool used in many research fields, has been fundamentally misused. Tests of statistical significance allow researchers to establish whether the results derived from study of a representative sample can confidently be generalised to the population on which it is based. For these authors, the problem lies in the use of the word 'whether', which they suggest is not a quantitative, scientific question, but rather a philosophical, qualitative one. They argue that statistical significance is based on a belief in calculability as the basis for decision making, without taking sufficient account of the purposes that such tests ought to serve. This critique of economics relates closely to management research, since it has been said that management research suffers from economics (March, 2000, cited in Grey, 2010: 684), as well as physics envy, mentioned earlier.

Ziliak and McCloskey describe contemporary economists committed to achieving statistical significance as 'cult members' who practise methodological rituals in strongly normative scholarly communities. This makes it almost impossible for anyone to question the orthodoxy of statistical significance. They argue that economists (and by extension other researchers who use statistical significance in the same way) have lost sight of the *meaning* of the results they generate through complex, computerised analyses of enormous databases. In other words, the size of the database, the number of observations, and the degree of statistical significance that the tests are able to show, have become more important than the substance of the findings.

Ziliak and McCloskey think of substance in two ways: first, as a way of understanding the economic importance of the research being conducted. They claim that many of their colleagues conduct research on issues which they *can*, rather than making decisions about what research *needs* to be done in order to enhance understanding. Consequently, research is led by the availability of suitable datasets or even the statistical tests themselves, instead of by what is thought to be interesting or an important problem that needs to be solved. Second, perhaps more importantly, it appears that many researchers sitting in dimly lit rooms staring at banks of computer screens waiting for statistical tests to churn out results have neglected to think about the meaning of the results. It is relatively easy to point to a statistically significant difference in, for example, the profitability of organisations that take different approaches to human resource management. It is much more difficult to say what this result means, for researchers, people in organisations, or the society in which the organisation is situated.

Ecological (in)validity

But this is not the only kind of issue that impedes the meaningfulness and relevance of positivist management research. Another arises from the high value placed on experimental research, as a means of controlling the variables within a research design so that the independent variable can be manipulated and tested. If this is done well, for example by dividing research subjects into treatment and control groups that can be compared, the study is presumed to be of high quality, due to the increased degree of confidence that researchers can have in assuming that any causal inferences made on the basis of differences between the two groups are accurate. However, it is extremely rare for experiments in management research to be carried out in the real world contexts of organisations. Instead, most are laboratory experiments, conducted in the context of the university, artificially creating an environment intended to simulate organisational conditions. The subjects involved in these experiments are not selected because they are managers or employees in a company or a public sector organisation. Instead they are usually (middle-class, highly educated) students on undergraduate or postgraduate business degree programmes. Research subjects are typically given a small amount of course credit as an incentive to participate in the study, or sometimes even a gift token.

To what extent can we be confident in the findings from such studies? Let us say that the study seeks to test the relationship between leadership style and employee creativity. Let's also say that the research subjects are German undergraduate students recruited from across various disciplines in the university. The experiment involves instructing participants to 'act like a trainee of a management consulting company' and generating 'ideas to increase customer satisfaction in supermarkets' (Herrmann and Felfe, 2012: 8). Here is an extract from the brief that research participants are given:

> Imagine you are a trainee of a management consulting firm... The secretary of the managing director has asked you to arrive at the conference room this morning... This morning you arrived at the conference room. Please imagine that you are currently in the conference room and that the other students with whom you are waiting are other trainees who have also been asked by the secretary of the managing director to attend to the meeting... the managing director will soon enter the room. (Herrmann and Felfe, 2012: 8)

To what extent are these students (whom we may assume to be young adults with relatively limited experience of work organisations) able to meaningfully imagine themselves into this situation, given that they are not and probably never have been management trainees, and may never have worked in a supermarket? Is it possible for researchers, through assigning students to work on simulated business tasks which they know to be unreal, where they are 'working' for a leader who is a paid male actor enacting a theoretically defined leadership role assigned to him by a researcher, to create a situation that is comparable to a real world organisation? If after the hour-long experiment, participants are presented with the statement 'my leader makes clear what one can expect to receive when performance goals are achieved', and asked whether or not they agree with it, do they have enough experience of the situation and the people involved to form a meaningful impression? If they are asked these questions by a professor whose class they are taking and where presumably they want to get a good grade, will they respond in the same way as they would if they were working for a large multinational organisation?

The answer is OF COURSE NOT! Because the simplified conditions of the classroom experiment never apply in real life. These are artificial contexts where participants are faced with simplified scenarios or tasks. These difficulties also extend beyond the classroom and include experimental research that does not involve students, such as the study by Butterfield et al. (2000) that involved sending practitioners a questionnaire by mail in which they were presented with scenarios (short descriptions of an ethically ambiguous situation) and asked what issues they felt were important in it. In organisations, no situation is ever anywhere near this simple. And yet a substantial amount of management research is done in this way and then generalised to 'real world' persons and situations. Even if such studies may be considered technically valid, they are severely limited in the extent to which they can provide meaningful insight into people's behaviour in their everyday lives. Or to use the terminology of research quality evaluation, they have very limited external and ecological validity. The problems with measuring the quality of management research using positivistic standards can be summarised using what is popularly known as the McNamara fallacy, after the US Secretary of Defence at the time of the Vietnam War:

> The first step is to measure whatever can be easily measured. This is OK as far as it goes. The second step is to disregard that which can't be easily measured or to give it an arbitrary quantitative value. This is artificial and misleading. The third step is to presume that what can't be measured easily really isn't important. This is blindness. The fourth step is to say that what can't be easily measured really doesn't exist. This is suicide. (quoted in Handy, 1994: 219)

Whether applied to the measurement of success in war or research, the principle remains the same – concentrating only on variables that can easily be seen and measured carries the risk that you radically underestimate the complexity of the situation. This is a classic instance of measuring what can be measured and potentially disregarding that which can't. In the final part of this chapter we turn to mixed methods, which is seen by some as a potential solution to the tensions between quantitative and qualitative research.

⬤⬤⬤⬤⬤⬤ Are the paradigm wars really over?

The four paradigm model developed by Burrell and Morgan and discussed in Chapter 3, has been very influential in management research and prompted a great deal of debate. Much of this focuses on the assertion that a researcher cannot operate in more than one paradigm at any given time, 'since in accepting the assumptions of one, we defy the assumptions of all the others' (Burrell and Morgan, 1979: 21). Burrell and Morgan argue that it is not possible for researchers to move between the paradigms, or even to talk meaningfully to researchers in different paradigms. They also argue that theories generated within one paradigm stand in fundamental opposition to theories produced in others. Researchers such as Hassard (1991), mentioned earlier, attempted to test this proposition by carrying out multiple paradigm research that illustrated their particularities and potential complementarity. Some suggested that the paradigm mentality was misleading and limiting to the possibilities of theorising organisation (Willmott, 1990). Others said that it was essential in protecting and opening up alternatives to the positivist orthodoxy in management research (Jackson and Carter, 1991).

More recently, it has been suggested the paradigm framework is less relevant as a means of understanding management research than it used to be. The distinction between subjective and objective research is seen as unhelpful because the relationship between structure and agency is widely understood as interconnected. In other words, 'people have a reflexive relationship with the world around them (i.e. they both constitute and are constituted by their surroundings)' (Cunliffe, 2011: 656). Burrell and Morgan's classification also distinguishes between critical (radical humanist and radical structuralist) and what they call interpretive sociological research, implying that the latter does not involve critique of things like power interests, an assertion that critical interpretive researchers challenge. As these criticisms illustrate, the heuristic device of Burrell and Morgan's two by two matrix should not be interpreted too rigidly, as the binary oppositions between radical and regulatory, subjective and objective, do not adequately encompass the full range of methodological possibilities available.

But in addition to ongoing debates about paradigmatic closure there is a growing view that paradigmatic distinctions are becoming less relevant in management research than several decades ago. This relates to the growth of interest in mixed methods research which involves combining quantitative and qualitative methods within the same study. Mixed methods are seen by some as offering the best of both worlds and have become something of a methodological fashion.

Alan Bryman, with whom Emma co-authors a methods textbook, has done a great deal to constructively explain mixed methods in management research, and in the social sciences more broadly. Bryman (2006) argues that the paradigm wars have largely subsided and discussions of epistemology and ontology become less prominent. This he suggests paves the way for a rapprochement between quantitative and qualitative methods, which may be more easily integrated without fear that this might be considered intellectually inconsistent. Mixed methods researchers often appeal pragmatically to the need to design a study using the methods that most effectively answer the research question, or suggest their choice is driven by the expectations of research funding bodies. But these methods choices come with their own disadvantages. For example, mixed methods research considerably increases the unpredictability of research outcomes, to the extent that the reason for combining them may result in quite different outcomes from those originally anticipated and researchers often underestimate the complexity associated with their use. Mixed methods research also raises issues about how to assess research quality when the criteria applied to the quantitative aspect of the study are likely to be different from those applied to the qualitative element.

But more important than this is that mixed methods are increasingly being seen by management researchers as a way of overcoming methodological and philosophical differences and making qualitative methods more acceptable in the context of the dominant positivist management research paradigm. Unlike Bryman, we do not see this as a sign that the paradigm wars are over. Instead there is a danger that the 'intellectual imperialism of the functionalist orthodoxy' (Willmott, 1990: 44) in management research becomes stronger, as alternatives are increasingly appropriated into neopositivist forms. While this is not a new threat (Burrell and Morgan referred to it back in 1979), it now assumes a different guise. Mixed methods offer the promise of a solution, but one that we are wary about. We are not inherently opposed to mixed methods. But we are concerned about the way in which mixed methods are being positioned as a solution to the problem of legitimacy and a way of transcending fundamental differences between management researchers – differences which in our view are essential to the diversity and richness of the field.

One way of addressing this problem might be to abandon the binary division of quantitative and qualitative methods. Yanow (2003) discusses the distinction between 'large n' and 'small n' research – with 'n' referring to the number of observations. The former involves statistical analysis of large amounts of numerical data. The latter refers to studies using non-statistical methods of field-based interviewing and observation (commonly thought of as qualitative research). But this distinction is spurious because small 'n' studies, like ethnography, typically involve a large number of observational encounters conducted over a considerable time period (Yanow and Schwartz-Shea, 2006). More importantly, the quantitative/qualitative distinction is used to refer to small 'n' studies that apply large 'n' tools (Yanow, 2003). Consequently, the interpretive basis of qualitative research is in danger of being lost, as qualitative researchers face growing pressure to conform to methodologically positivist norms. Yanow therefore favours a tripartite distinction between quantitative, positivist-qualitative and interpretive, qualitative methods.

Conclusion

The issues discussed in this chapter affect all areas of management research, from accounting and marketing to organisation studies and strategy. In all these sub-fields, positivist values about quality tend to dominate and many new researchers are wary about using qualitative research methods. This can encourage isomorphism and conservatism in methods choice, rather than innovation in trying to find new ways of creating knowledge.

John Law (2004), quoted at the start of this chapter, suggests that methodological rule-following has resulted in the predominance of a particular version of rigour in social science which emphasises the importance of obtaining technically robust accounts of reality using conventional research methods. The problem with this, he suggests, is that methods practices are performative – not only do they *describe* reality, they also help to *produce* it. Another problem with this is that it fails to acknowledge the dazzling complexity of reality. He therefore argues that we need to unlearn our automatic use of method and become more modest in our quest for understanding, and more willing to live with uncertainty. We need to see research as a process of crafting realities, based on finding and making patterns and gaining insights into one thing by making other things absent. Law is careful to point out that he is not advocating a descent into relativism, wherein there is no point in using conventional research methods to study the world. Rather, he is saying that the vital importance of research in shaping and changing our world means we need to be more flexible in trying to understand it. There is thus an ethical basis to his argument.

To illustrate the difference between an ethically based and an instrumentally driven approach to methods, we end with a story. Recently

Emma attended a research seminar where a management researcher was presenting his work. The study was about leadership, which is something that interests her, and the ideas were thought provoking. But there was something about the researchers' approach to study that was puzzling. As he spoke, it became clear that there were a lot of different methods and methodological terms being used. Some of these concepts were aligned with a positivist viewpoint; others were more interpretive in orientation. Throughout, the speaker kept referring to where he might seek to publish his work. When he finished the presentation, Emma asked him about his research methods, and whether he could clarify a little more his philosophical and methodological position. The speaker responded by saying he was entirely pragmatic, and that it depended on which journal he decided to submit the article to for publication; if it was a more positivistically oriented journal, he would beef up this aspect of the methodology, whereas for a journal more sympathetic to interpretive research, he would slant the methodology towards this. This account illustrates a highly pragmatic approach to methods choice. We find this worrying because it appears to contain no inherent ethic beyond individual career success, for example by getting published in the 'right' journal. Our view is that methods choice should be driven by underlying ethical commitments – an issue we will return to shortly.

5

Theory in Management Research

Nothing is so practical as a good theory. (Kurt Lewin, 1945, cited in Van de Ven, 1989: 486)

This chapter is concerned with the process of theorising. Interestingly, it is surprisingly difficult to say what theorising really is, or even what constitutes theory in management research, despite the fact that generating theory is the primary goal of research. The importance of this issue in management research therefore cannot be underestimated. And yet some have argued that we don't train students adequately in theory construction. Consequently, it is feared that there are just not enough members of the research community who 'have that ineffable something that makes a good theorist' (Sutton and Staw, 1995)! Why does this matter? Is it because research careers are influenced by our ability to publish research in elite academic journals, which require new contributions to theory (Sutton and Staw, 1995; Rynes, 2005; Colquitt and Zapata-Phelan, 2007)?

We often take for granted what we, as social scientists and management scholars, mean by theory. Here we take theory to be a 'unified, systematic explanation' of phenomena that is explanatory and empirical (Schwandt, 1997: 154). Theory-building can be said to be three activities – 'creating, constructing and justifying a theory' (Van de Ven, 2007: 141). But even if we know what theory is, there are differences of opinion about the point in the research process when theory should be developed. For example, grounded theorists are of the view that theoretical ideas should only be developed *after* the data has been collected, and theory should *not* be used to formulate hypotheses or develop research questions prior to data collection. However, latterly, writers like Charmaz (2005) have encouraged a move away from the idea that grounded theory involves the researcher entering the research scene without a frame of reference. And most other researchers assume that theory shapes the interpretation of data to a greater or lesser extent.

One person who was particularly concerned with theory was the researcher Kurt Lewin, who studied group dynamics, leadership and learning (Van de Ven and Poole, 1995). Lewin was influential in setting up a kind of laboratory for studying human behaviour in the 1940s. The lab pioneered a small-group discussion method, called T-group, which involved people participating in decision making and simultaneously analysing each other's behaviour, all of which was recorded by the researchers. Lewin believed that even complex social phenomena like organisations could be understood through close and detailed observation, which in turn could enable identification of consistent patterns of human behaviour (Lewin, 1951). He is widely credited with the quote at the start of this chapter. What we understand Lewin to mean by this aphorism is that management theory should not be about developing complex, abstract theoretical models that an intelligent, thoughtful worker or manager would find difficult to relate to their lived experience. Rather, it should be about developing and using theory as a catalyst for meaningful change: a goal that contains an ethical and political dimension.

On maps and navigation

One way of thinking about research is as a foreign terrain made up of challenging features that the researcher has to navigate. Harburg's (1966) island of research (or research map) – which you can look up on the internet if you are interested – offers a light-hearted take on the trials and tribulations that researchers often face in their research. It shows the researcher emerging from the 'Sea of Theory' onto the land. They then have to navigate a wide variety of challenges including the 'Problem Mountain Range' and the 'Canyon of Despair', which give way to the 'Wreck Heap of Discarded Hypotheses' and 'The Great Fundless Desert'. Eventually they re-enter the sea of theory – after traversing the 'Bog of Lost Manuscripts' and the 'Delta of Editors', (depicting the difficulties faced in writing up). One of the reasons we like this image, is because it illustrates how we immerse ourselves in theory at the beginning of the research process and then build on it based on our experiences. What we read and those issues that appear important then become central during data collection, and then we return to theory at the end to frame a contribution to the literature. At this point we either confirm what is already known or, more satisfyingly, identify aspects in the research that are either new or surprising, or both.

But despite the importance of theorising, the actual process is often left as an unspoken part of the journey (see Van de Ven, 2007, Chapter 4, for a rare example). It is supposed to be the most exciting and difficult part of the research process, but is one on which many writers are silent. One reason for this relates to the difficulty of deciding what exactly a theory is, and what must be done to demonstrate a 'theoretical contribution'. In thinking about and writing this book, we found precious little in research methods books in management (including our own) that deal with this issue. The result is that postgraduate students (including PhD candidates) aren't always familiar with the tools or skills needed to start the important task of theory development. The map is useful, but we also need to know how to navigate and why we're making the journey.

Acquiring and selecting theoretical lenses: trends and pressures

Theory development is made more difficult by confusion surrounding the importance placed on the use of theoretical lenses, as well as understanding where the theorising process fits into the research act. In particular, do researchers always have to have a meta-theoretical position from which they conduct their work, and, if they do, which one should they choose? It has long been known that informal groups play a considerable part in the socio-cognitive structuring of the way research fields develop, such that trends or fashions occur. These trends in turn influence the theoretical lenses used (Vogel, 2012). Such groups also shape the way in which researchers, for example PhD students, acquire the theories they use. What is possible in terms of theory, therefore, depends in part on the interests and experience of their supervisors, other research students, and the interests of journal editors who are themselves usually loosely connected to the establishment and promotion of certain perspectives – in other words the community of practice. In recent years, the issue of theory development has become even more important as even doctoral students and early-career researchers are expected to declare their theoretical perspective and contribute to debates in academic journals from the very start of their careers.

Theorising: the 'dark art' of management research?

Some management researchers we talk to (some well into their working lives as scholars) tell us that they 'have always struggled at theory-building'. Theorising is sometimes thought of as how to learn to do the miraculous, repeatedly. Where the miracle occurs is also where serendipity happens, along with surprises, new insights, and ultimately the development of theory. But how can more management researchers learn to perform miracles (or at least be around to observe them happening)? We think that the 'dark art' of theory-building can be better articulated, even if few supervisors are confident enough in describing the process and the practice. This goes beyond suggesting that people read 'What Constitutes a Theoretical Contribution' (Whetten, 1989) or 'Appealing Work' (Golden-Biddle and Locke, 1993), excellent as both of these are. A number of questions that relate to building theory continually crop up, such as: how does new theory integrate with existing theories? How can understanding of a construct or phenomenon be deepened? How can better understandings of relationships between constructs be achieved? When is it appropriate to scrap an existing theory and start again?

One student we taught told us she had been advised to 'sit in the steam room and think more about your theory'. Another said he had been told that theory-building would yield a kind of 'eureka moment' (in the bath, perhaps?), whilst another suggested that his understanding was of 'a creative and flexible process where time is needed for an activity in which you are intimately connected for this [theory] to unfold' – which sounds a little mystical. Taken together, these pieces of advice are interesting because they reinforce the idea that research is a craft that needs to be practiced. It also emphasises that there is (or might be) an element of serendipity. Building theory may not be a predictable process whereby the desired outcome will simply come by following a set of rules or a linear process, as researchers believed prior to Weick's paper on 'disciplined imagination' (Weick, 1989; Cornelissen, 2006). If serendipity is involved, then it may be that most people learning to practice research as a craft are neither well equipped with skills nor clear about the approaches available to construct theory. In order to develop such skills, it is important to first understand what theories actually do in more detail, and the elements they consist of.

What theory does (and what it doesn't do)

So what does a theory do? Locke (2001: 35) suggests that theories give meaning to the world via a 'constructed set of interrelated propositions', which – through the insights of the researcher – serve to make sense of particular observed events. Although this at first glance appears useful, Sayer (1984: 48) suggests that theory as a concept is used in a highly 'elastic' manner, both in social science and in everyday life. He suggests that common-sense conceptions of what theory is highlight a number of important contrasts that should not be ignored. For example, contrasts of theory as fact or reality, practice or common sense, speculative or certain.

DiMaggio (1995) takes a similar view and suggests three perspectives on theory, each of which has some strengths and certain limitations:

1   The first perspective suggests that theory provides some *covering laws*. These generalisations, when taken together, describe and explain some phenomenon or part of it. These are often summarised as relationships between variables (Campbell, 1990; Colquitt and Zapata-Phelan, 2007).
2   The second perspective sees a theory as a vehicle to enlightenment. In line with this view, DiMaggio (1995) suggests that theory is necessarily complex, defamiliarising and *rich in paradox*. Further, enlightenment in this form comes not from conceptual clarity and the ability to use it to generalise, but rather from the element of surprise that emanates from *exciting insights*.
3   The third perspective suggests that theory provides a narrative (DiMaggio, 1995). Here, the idea is that the descriptions offered can account for social processes, provided empirical evidence underpins the narrative for particular perspectives and circumstances, and the account offered (see also Eisenhardt, 1989).

Others have suggested that theories can be:

- *normative*: specifying what work managers should do, and how;
- *descriptive*: describing what managers do in practice;
- *analytical*: emphasising particular aspects of management at the expense of others, e.g. a critical perspective;
- *simplifying*: aiming not to dazzle academics with the complexity and detail of the empirical world (Bacharach, 1989).

In 1995, the *Academy of Management Journal* ran a series of articles on theory that specifically discussed what it is not (DiMaggio, 1995; Sutton et al., 1995; Weick, 1995). From this, we learn that these scholars think theory is not references, data, lists of variables, diagrams or hypotheses – though they believe it is closely related to these things, drawing them together and providing the understanding for the links.

Concepts: the building blocks of theory

Denzin (1989) takes this further by arguing that it is through the ordering of concepts that a schema is developed. This can then be used to explain a phenomenon in the world. Within a schema, the development and identification of concepts become instrumental activities, as concepts shape the content of the theories and help us to see new explanations. Locke (2001) suggests that it is through the concepts identified and grouped by the researcher into 'data documents' that we achieve a sense of what things link with what other things, which are discrete, and which are unhelpful or misunderstood. Thus, concepts do two things simultaneously: they provide new ways of looking at the world, and they bring some new aspect of the world into existence through conceptualisation. But we also have to think about what a 'good' concept is, as well as what they are useful for. Social scientist John Gerring (1999) argued that we could work to a set of quality criteria in assessing concepts, whatever field of social research we practice. These criteria are: familiarity, resonance, parsimony, coherence, differentiation, depth, theoretical utility and field utility. These are worth thinking about in a bit more detail.

'Familiarity' refers to how easily a concept is understood by the audience. As Gerring emphasises, the audience could be academically trained or lay (that is, non-expert). If the concept is familiar, then it will most likely also achieve resonance with, or be meaningful to, the audience. A concept is more likely to be resonant if it is parsimonious – in other words, relatively short as a term and in its immediate clarification. Alongside this, as you would expect, the concept must be internally coherent – if it contradicts itself empirically or in its description, then it is not a good concept. In addition, readers or listeners (and, most essentially, reviewers!) must be able to see what differentiates the concept being developed from other concepts. If it's not different, then why spend time and energy developing it? Then, in an ideal world, the concept should have depth, theoretical utility in its ability to generate further research or explain other empirical phenomena, and relevance to the wider field of research, however defined.[1]

This is an interesting set of criteria to consider. However, what makes Gerring's argument especially interesting is his insistence that concept formation is not something that anyone can achieve simply by working through his list. Instead, it is a very unpredictable process during which the researcher has to navigate (and here we think again of the map at the start of the chapter), making compromises in considering each criterion. As with other aspects of the research process, the formal frontstage description can mask the messiness of the action backstage.

Where do theories come from?

In thinking about concept formation and the development of theory, there is one other key question: should researchers identify a dominant focus (i.e. one theory), or be open to a multiplicity of theories? Some argue that the research community needs a 'toolbox' of theories, noting that all theoretical tools bring their own specific limitations (summarised in the proverb, 'If you only have a hammer, you tend to see every problem as a nail'). Thinking about which theories to use will probably involve examining the relationship with other researchers around you, including your supervisor – who is probably the person telling you most forcefully what good theory is, or how to develop concepts. However, most of us are also keen to explore new shores, maybe using a different map – otherwise, why would we have become researchers? The supervision of research, again in an ideal world, navigates between orthodoxy and creativity.

Organisation theorist Mike Reed (1992) offers a range of analytical frameworks, or theoretical positions, each focusing on different problems. Each framework, he suggests, provides a basis for its associated conceptual development, and indicates the link to the approaches that might be taken to research. For example, systems theory has taken as its central problem the adaptation of internal organisation structures that occurs through changes in a range of environmental factors. By providing an understanding of these complex processes and the way in which organisations adapt and change to environmental pressures, systems theory gives management useful information as to how it can change and adapt to remain effective.

Another analytical framework identified is the negotiated-order perspective, which begins slightly 'further back' in an attempt to uncover how organisation itself takes place, or is constructed and maintained. Other frameworks include power and domination perspectives, which examine the political and economic structures through which control is exercised; cultural and symbolic perspectives, which seek mainly to understand how a collective sense of organisational identity is maintained; and practice perspectives, which identify a range of social agencies that come together to achieve particular objectives.

In recent years there has been a movement to require explanation of the theoretical position taken, as an additional means of linking methodology and methods. As management is a relatively young discipline, one argument says that a failure to always do this is related to a lack of understanding of the relationship to 'meta-theory'. To some extent, the perspective taken depends on the disciplinary roots on which the researcher is drawing – economists, for example, would approach a topic in a very different way from sociologists. Vogel (2012) discusses the notion of 'invisible colleges' within management and organisation studies. These colleges to some extent provide the theoretical lenses through which researchers conduct their work. Of course, the theoretical lens chosen forms only one component in framing the question; other aspects, for example the empirical qualities of the issue under study, are also extremely important. Whilst appearing reasonably static, all analytical approaches are highly fluid and dynamic. However, patterns of college development and transformation can be traced. Vogel does this from the early 1990s to the present day, showing how the dominant focus on contingency theory in the 1980s died away, whilst other approaches – such as organisational symbolism and behavioural theory – maintained their visibility over three decades within key journals.

Surprise, surprise! Or, what makes an interesting theoretical contribution?

It's fine to understand what a theory is, how it is related to concepts, and the social process of theory development. But how do leading theories emerge? What makes some theories so popular? This brings us to another quest that preoccupies scholars: to unearth the secrets of what makes a good theoretical contribution (Bergh, 2003). A piece of research can provide many different kinds of contribution (Colquitt and Zapata-Phelan, 2007). One that might not be immediately obvious is surprise.

Hillman outlines theory-building through a similar kind of metaphor. A unifying theme that links why different types of theory have been particularly successful in social science has been why and how they have surprised the audience. The notion of surprise is a useful way of thinking about what the outcome of research should be. Sayer (1984) suggests that theoretical surprises can be divided into various types:

1   discovery of surprising new objects, which suggest the previous conceptualisation of a phenomenon may not in fact be sufficient;
2   a development in, rather than just growth of, an idea, such that the existing concept undergoes surprising changes in meaning;
3   a discovery made through surprisingly failing to meet expectations – for example, a contradiction of expected results or practices, due to conceptual failure or the failure of associated techniques that have framed the way we have previously understood the relationship between observations made and theoretical statements derived;
4   changes in the structure of conceptual systems – a process that mostly happens through theoretical reflection, where surprising inconsistencies are uncovered, whether in quantitative equations or from misunderstanding or mislabelling concepts.

Sayer's way of thinking about theory through the idea of surprise was echoed, or presaged, in a journal article published in 1971 by the philosopher Murray Davis. You can get a sense of his argument from the title, 'That's Interesting!' – and also from the final line, 'So what? Who cares?' (Davis, 1971: 344). In-between, Davis leads us through a fascinating argument: that the best sociological theories are those that challenge assumptions the audience brings to the topic being researched. In doing this, Davis takes us away from the idea that the best theories have to be *true*; they may be – but that is not the purpose of theory-building in the social sciences. Instead, the truth-value of a theory should be secondary (according to Davis) to its *interest*. This is a theme picked up in a slightly different way by Locke et al. (2008). By drawing on notions of abduction and the work of Peirce, they argue that by overemphasising the process of validation the degree of imagination and self-belief necessary for good theorising becomes overly reduced.

Textbooks on methods and their 'how to' guides, according to Davis, will generate only *dull* theories. They may be technically competent, but they will disappear into history largely unacknowledged. Engaging theories, on the other hand, will probably come from researchers who question what everyone else takes for granted, in a kind of 'breaching' (Garfinkel, 1967) process (because the theory breaks into the reality that is assumed). This is an argument of great importance to us here, because it suggests that minute developments of established existing theories will be a) dull and b) not very helpful as a way of increasing understanding. It emphasises the miraculous – but Davis is also good enough to suggest ways of training yourself to find miracles more easily.

Standing – or dancing – on the shoulders of giants

As Davis (1971) also emphasises, the process that researchers go through in order to deal with the *bit in the middle* – to develop interesting theory – is closely linked to practice, methodology, the concepts you use, how you define them, and how you bring them together in some kind of order to make sense of the world. At the end of the day, theory needs to be grounded in good academic labour, about which we already know, but at the same time presented in a way that surprises us. This is not an easy task, because we are required to look over the shoulders of all those who have gone before and created the concepts, theories and ideas we now review, whilst also trying to be creative and open to something new that we may not quite believe to begin with. It is difficult to read and be respectful of what has gone before, whilst at the same time be creative: as one doctoral student put it, it's like 'learning to dance, rather than stand, on the shoulders of giants'. For many, it's too easy to be defensive, rather like driving an armoured vehicle so as not to get injured in a collision.

Theory from start to finish

Some management researchers choose their theory at the same time as their methodology. Here are some examples to show how the theory you select shapes the methods you use, the level of analysis that you focus on (individual, group, organisational or societal), the data collected, and ultimately the kind of knowledge you're able to develop. There is an element of determinism here, in the sense that the theoretical choices you make determine the methods that constitute the 'right tool for the job':

- Engaging with Goffman's theory of presentation of self in everyday life has methodological implications for the kind of data collected (microsituational interactions between organisational actors) and ways of collecting it (participant observation and fieldnotes).
- Starting with activity theory a) has implications for identifying subjects and objects within the study, and b) suggests that data focus on communities of practice, divisions of labour within the organisation,

power relationships, and various aspects relating to means, use of language, systems and procedures, and organisational infrastructure.

- Working with institutional theory has methodological implications through focusing on how regulatory framework and national policies form, shape, enable and link particular activities and behaviours. Methodologically, it also implies a need to understand national economic policy and political influence.

- Finally, Foucauldian theory, within which power and knowledge are seen as constituted through discourses of discipline and control, suggests critical discourse analysis (usually analysing texts, whether naturally occurring or interview-based) to understand how those discourses were constructed and the effects they had.

Finding the right – or a good-enough – pair of glasses

It's probably becoming clear by now that the notion of 'having a theoretical lens' is appealing in part because it helps to delimit the nature of the problem and the way the study is conducted. Richard's early research work was conducted within a context that emphasised the contingency theory framework; management researchers were trying to identify contingent variables (behavioural, structural and environmental) that would predict the success of different kinds of payment scheme. Inspired by a number of industrial anthropologists, particularly Donald Roy and Tom Lupton, Richard's chosen perspective related closely to the methodologies adopted (participant observation and field notes), and latterly to content analysis of the data. Emma, on the other hand, began her research career in a social context where cultural approaches were becoming dominant, as a way of exploring power and control in organisations. Her methodology was also case-based, and her methods centred on observation and interview data, in trying to understand how the experience of payment systems had changed (or stayed the same).

A colleague of ours, interested in knowledge in small firms, adopted an activity theoretical approach. This position sees organisations as based on agendas that are mediated through a variety of means (symbols, language and the systems of an organisation), as well as through the communities of practice with which the organisation members relate, and organisational rules, norms and divisions of labour. The approach also seeks to understand how these various dimensions have come into being, culturally and historically. The approach, as might be imagined, requires information and data to be collected about many issues, from a wide range of organisational stakeholders. The activity systems approach suggests that action and understanding come from agents working to produce certain outcomes.

Perhaps a different approach to the issue of lens would be helpful here: let's think about the most famous lens in the world – that belonging to Sherlock Holmes. In an exercise that we use with students, we show a short clip from a film. In this scene, Sherlock is examining a bowler hat. Holmes hands it to Watson to see what he makes of it; Watson announces he can see nothing. Holmes then sets about describing the characteristics and personality of the person who has worn this hat: for example, the man is not fit, his wife has ceased to love him, he was a man of foresight who has for some reason fallen on more difficult times due to some evil influence, he is a drinker, he has no gaslight in his house, and he has had his hair cut in the last two or three days.

Watson is, as usual, amazed by this display of brilliance. He asks Holmes how he can justify the claims being made. It becomes clear that Holmes is developing theories, tested with a limited amount of data on the hat. More interestingly, Holmes makes the process explicit, telling Watson (and the viewer) how he forms his deductions. Holmes is a true polymath. For example, he uses social theory to explain why he believes the man's wife has ceased to love him – the hat has not been brushed for many weeks. This suggests the marriage is failing because responsibility for this kind of domestic maintenance in nineteenth-century London lay with the woman. Following this, Holmes also uses psychological theories, related to risk: '…the man has taken the trouble to purchase a secure to prevent this relatively expensive hat from being blown off by the wind, but the secure has been broken and he has not taken the trouble to replace it.'[2] Contemporary medical science is invoked to explain that the individual is intellectual (the hat being large), and is not in the habit of exercising (the lining showing evidence of perspiration).

This is a fascinating section of film, partly because some of the 'facts' that Holmes confidently asserts have been shown to be wrong. Yet the explanations of how Holmes forms his theory are still convincing. In addition, his theoretical work is comprehensible only if the explanation is seen in its proper cultural and historical context. In terms of the number of glasses we might use and how these might relate to such things as the way the metatheoretical positioning links to the way we craft persuasive research accounts. Cunliffe (2011) has suggested that developments in organisational theory and research methods as well as ways of theorising has meant that choices (specifically in relation to qualitative methods) have become far more complex. One last thing to keep in mind in choosing glasses is the idea that all researchers imagine and construe theoretical representations in their own way. This means that different researchers are likely to come up with different theoretical representations, even though the general topic of the research may be the same. Their educational and cultural backgrounds, as well as previous research experiences, all affect the way in which researchers view a research topic conceptually. In describing the process of conceptualising her research topic, one research student told us of the anxiety she felt when told by her supervisor that she needed to have some kind of 'conceptual model' to frame her research. In the end, she decided to build on a theoretical model that had been developed by her supervisor and, through engaging with different literatures, to extend it by adding new elements to the model. She used this as the basis for her research question and hypotheses, which informed her empirical study. Having a conceptual model is not meant to restrict, merely to guide and align thinking into more productive channels. The student said she found many new and different avenues to follow in her research, but it did help to have a guiding model that kept the project focused.

Disciplined imagination and the art of making choices

Throughout this chapter, we've emphasised that formulating ideas about an issue (theory development) can be understood as a process. American social psychologist and organisation theorist Karl Weick (1989) characterises this as *disciplined imagination*. This is an alternative to the approach sometimes referred to as 'gap spotting', inspired by the natural sciences model of research, mentioned earlier. Building on some of the ideas we have already discussed in relation to creativity in research (which might lead to a conceptual breakthrough), we believe Weick's views are useful here. When researchers think about a subject or problem, they imagine various ways of viewing and operationalising this (the 'imagination' element) before making a decision on one or a range of perspectives (the 'disciplined' element) that they adopt and elaborate on in the research. Weick likens this process to artificial selection, as 'theorists are both the source of variation and the source of selection' (Weick, 1989: 520) when they imagine and decide on theoretical perspectives and ideas in relation to a particular subject or problem.

Weick also suggests that disciplined imagination is characterised by simultaneous rather than sequential thinking, and revolves around three components: problem statements, thought trials and selection criteria. These components represent reference points in the process where researchers can act differently and produce theories of better quality or more interest. As Weick (1989: 529) remarks,

> theory construction can be modified at the step where the problem is stated (make assumptions more explicit, make representation more accurate, make representation more detailed), at the step where thought trials are formulated (increase number of trials generated, increase heterogeneity of trials generated), and at the step where criteria select among thought trials (apply criteria more consistently, apply more criteria simultaneously, apply more diverse criteria).

The implication of Weick's argument, reiterated by Cornelissen (2006), is that researchers need to engage in a series of mental experiments or thought trials where they iterate between reviewed literature, preliminary analyses, background assumptions, and their own intuition, to consider a variety of metaphors, ideas and models as representations of the subject or problem in hand ('imagination') before selecting and deciding upon one metaphorical image that serves as a starting point for further inquiry ('disciplined'). Research for Weick involves a combination of deductive reasoning, based upon a reading of the available literature on the topic, and inductive reasoning, through intuitive and creative thinking.

Another significant implication of Weick's thinking is that it suggests an active role for researchers who imagine or construe theoretical representations, rather than seeing such theoretical representations as deductively or naturally following on from a literature review. Disciplined imagination is therefore rooted in the view that the 'logic' of research and the process of theory construction is creative, social and psychological: it is a matter of heuristics and associative thinking. Research and theorising are, therefore, more like artificial than natural selection as 'the theorist rather than nature intentionally guides the evolutionary process' (Weick, 1989: 519) of selecting new ideas and theoretical representations.

Scope, generalisation and the general theory of hole digging

If theories are to be useful, it is important that the claims made in respect to their generalisability are clearly stated. Easterby-Smith et al.

(2008) suggest that the requirement for generalisation may be either *descriptive*, where the researcher wishes to demonstrate that the characteristics of one setting are similar to or the same as another, or *theoretical*, where the ideas developed within one context are transferable and relevant to other contexts. Consider the example below in relation to hole digging.

> There once was a man who aspired to be the author of the general theory of holes. When asked 'What kind of hole – holes dug by children in the sand for amusement, holes dug by gardeners to plant lettuce seedlings, tank traps, holes made by road makers?' he would reply indignantly that he wished for a general theory that would explain all of these. He rejected *ab initio* the – as he saw it – pathetically common-sense view that of the digging of different kinds of holes there are quite different kinds of explanations to be given; why then he would ask do we have the concept of a hole? Lacking the explanations to which he originally aspired, he then fell to discovering statistically significant correlations; he found for example that there is a correlation between the aggregate hole-digging achievement of a society as measured, or at least one day to be measured, by econometric techniques, and its degree of technological development. The United States surpasses both Paraguay and Upper Volta in hole-digging; there are more holes in Vietnam than there were. These observations, he would always insist, were neutral and value-free. This man's achievement has passed totally unnoticed except by me. Had he however turned his talents to political science, had he concerned himself not with holes, but with modernization, urbanization or violence, I find it difficult to believe that he might not have achieved high office in the APSA. (MacIntyre, 1971: 260)

The point of this example, apart from telling us lots of interesting things about holes, is that it illustrates that when theories become too general and too abstract, they cease to be able to explain anything very much.

The practice of data analysis and theorising

What is perhaps becoming clear throughout this chapter is that as Locke (2011) has argued, explanation of the practices involved in theorising occupy very little space in any discussion on theory building. Under the heading 'practice' she argues too little attention is paid to processes such as conjecture and how researchers go about interpreting the observations they make.

Phillips and Pugh (2005) suggest that there are a number of features that distinguish good research from consultancy (a theme discussed in Chapter 1). One is maintaining, as far as possible, an 'open system of thought'. To achieve this Locke suggests, involves skills to abstract, compare, contrast and relate what is found in the data to what is already known, as well as being able to be surprised by what is found so that new ideas can be developed, even if there is little to support them. The rigour and consistency of this process is often helped at this stage by the use of 'tools' such as the creation of codes and categories, or the careful framing of the study through making explicit the assumptions made, for example through hypotheses or models – if these are appropriate to the style of the research. Whatever the conventions used, researchers are required to develop an approach that will be receptive to the unexpected. For example, in quantitative research designs, the early analysis of frequencies and cross tabulations will sometimes lead to the (unexpected) discovery of relationships that lend themselves to the development of important theoretical developments, whereas in building hypotheses it is useful if you consciously explore how they might be refuted and again be prepared to be surprised. As Locke indicates, the practice of building good theory requires a balance to be struck between actively working with the data and stepping back from the empirical analysis to read further around the issues that arise, and always being ready to see links and allow interpretations to unfold. As Phillips and Pugh (2005) advise, critically review the evidence behind the conclusions drawn by others and as Law (1994) describes it, be willing to look for information that will disconfirm what you already believe to be the case.

Conclusion

This chapter has dealt with the important issue of theory in management research, including what theorising really is and why it matters. We began by emphasising that we engage with theory at all stages of the research process, at the beginning when we examine what has gone before, when we chose the lens(es) through which we collect and analyse our data and build theory at the end of the process. The chapter also examined what theory is and what theory is not, before discussing the importance that surprise plays and some of the personal qualities that researchers need to develop to maximise the opportunities for theory development.

One crucial issue for those wishing to understand how to develop theory in management research is the importance of reading around the subject area where your interests lie. The message from this chapter is that new theory and theory development will more often than not come from novel linkages that can be made between ideas or from another field or discipline. This will bring challenge and novelty to the way the components of theory come together. This involves valuing the insights and approaches that emerge from such things as, wider reading, the use of multiple theoretical lenses (and assumptions), and reflecting and thinking whilst crafting your own theory.

Notes

1   As mentioned earlier, it is fashionable nowadays to see journal articles in management as the only form of outputs that 'count'. But books and chapters in books and other outlets for the generation of new theory (as stated by Barley, 2006; Colquitt and Zapata-Phelan, 2007) can also be important, perhaps for the very reason that there is often a need to have plenty of space to explain the theory, but also because of the well-known role of reviewers in blocking/rejecting new theory.

2   Taken from a *Sherlock Holmes* episode in the Granada Television series, 1984.

6

Who Are We to Do This?

> An important function of reflexive analysis is to expose the under-
> lying assumptions on which arguments and stances are built. We
> are socialized into assumptions as we internalize world views, world
> hypotheses, cultures, cosmologies, thought styles or paradigms.
> (Ray Holland, 1999: 467)

So far we have seen that management research is a messy process
which is carried out by people who have complex organisational, historical, political, ethical, evidential and personal reasons for doing it
(Buchanan and Bryman, 2007). It is therefore difficult to maintain a
view of the management researcher as a neutral observer. This is partly
because management research is close to practice, often undertaken by
researchers who at some point in their lives, perhaps even at the same
time, are also practising managers earning a living based on managerial
work. It should come as little surprise then that management research
is sometimes suggested to be more partial than some other research
disciplines.

This raises complex ethical and methodological issues concerning the
motives and values of the researcher and their relationship to the subject
they study. As a result, rather than being focused on studying someone
or something that is 'dramatically different' from themselves (as were the
social anthropologists of the early twentieth century who travelled to
distant lands to study 'exotic' cultures), management researchers focus
on people and things that are highly familiar to them and shape their
experience of the world every day. Not only does the proximity between
research and practice affect how studies are conducted, it influences
what is considered worth studying in the first place.

There are two possible responses to this situation. One is to try to
remove, or at least limit the influence of the researcher on the research
process. This is referred to as the reduction of a source of bias. As we
have already said, some researchers, especially those working in the
positivist tradition, assume it is possible to achieve scientific distance
and maintain neutrality in the research context in order to create
objective knowledge. But examples like the Hawthorne studies

emphasise the difficulties of doing this in situations involving people, who may be acutely aware that they are being studied and behave differently as a consequence.

The second possibility involves recognising that knowledge is affected by the personal beliefs, values and assumptions of the researcher and then trying to find ways of working ethically and productively within these constraints. This is the dominant stance within the interpretive traditions, including many critical approaches. There are also variations within this, for example constructionists are more inclined to see themselves as part of the research process, influencing the behaviour of the people they are studying simply by involving themselves in their lives, whereas constructivists hold a more objectivist view of research, seeing it as something that they can stand apart from (see Gergen, 1999). But to a greater or lesser extent all of these traditions invite consideration of what is referred to as reflexivity in the research process, an idea that will be discussed in this chapter. The goal therefore, is not the removal of bias, but rather 'perspectival subjectivity' through which the researcher becomes aware of how their interpretations are shaped and does their utmost to guard against the selective use of data to support prior assumptions (Sandberg, 2005).

Recently, there has also been growing attention devoted to the ethics of management research. This is partly driven by a desire among those who fund and support management research, including governments and universities that pay the salaries of researchers, to manage and avoid certain risks. Such risks include the possibility of complaint or legal action taken by organisations or individuals unhappy with the way they are portrayed in a study. The heightened emphasis on ethics could also be seen as part of a wider trend towards societal mistrust of professional occupations and a consequent desire to regulate their conduct, rather than to rely on professional self-regulation.

The issue of whether researchers can be trusted to behave ethically was highlighted by a case in 2009 involving a group at the University of East Anglia in the UK who were studying climate change. This involved an incident where the computer used by the researchers was hacked into and thousands of emails leaked onto the internet. It was suggested that some of the emails implied that the researchers had deliberately manipulated and suppressed data that was not supportive of their views on climate change in advance of an important international conference on the subject, the Copenhagen Summit. While the researchers vigorously refuted this assertion, saying that their email conversations had been taken out of context, the case highlighted a growing desire to hold researchers to account regarding their motives and ethics, particularly when the subject of study has major political and social implications. As this also emphasises, questions of ethics are relevant to *all* forms of research, and not just qualitative studies, or those involving face-to-face interaction between researcher and research participants.

In this chapter we turn our attention towards who we are as management researchers, how this shapes our approach to doing research, and how we might try to take account of our self identity in a way that is scientifically defensible, both to ourselves and others. It is important not to see this as an inwardly focused exercise, a narcissistic navel-gazing project in which you spend large amounts of time scrutinising your motives and practices, potentially to the point where you are put off actually getting on and doing any research at all. This chapter invites you to reflect on your personal beliefs, motives and values and how they guide you towards asking particular research questions and undertaking particular research projects. This immensely practical skill can help you to spot potential problems, and avoid getting into situations that potentially undermine the value of your work in broader organisational and societal contexts. Rather than being seen as an optional extra, we see ethical reflexivity as going to the heart of what it means to be a management researcher.

Taking sides

In the title of an article written in 1967, the sociologist Howard Becker asked the deceptively simple question, 'whose side are we on?' This formed the basis for interrogation of his research community's ethics and motives. Becker's question has been interpreted by radical social scientists to imply that a researcher's findings will always be evaluated ideologically by those in power, and accusations of bias are likely to be levelled at them if their findings are critical of established interests. For this reason, they argue, the question of bias cannot be avoided; researchers should simply choose whose side they are on.

Becker's article has also been read as a statement of epistemological radicalism, through implying that all research is biased in one way or another, as there is no objectively neutral position from which the social world can be viewed and commented upon (Hammersley, 2001). This can lead to the position of extreme relativism, associated with postmodernism and mentioned earlier, in which scientific research is seen as a 'language game' (Rorty, 1979; Latour, 1987). It involves rejection of the idea that research results are a direct representation of empirical facts or reality, and instead sees research as based on the use of certain conventions to build a convincing interpretation or story.

These arguments are highly applicable to management research because of the complex issues relating to purpose and relevance mentioned earlier. But unlike sociologists of deviance such as Becker, management researchers are often seen as on the side of the powerful, rather than the powerless. Yet many management researchers, including scholars of industrial relations, sociologists of work and labour process theorists who focus on the experience of employees as well as managers, would see this as a misrepresentation. This has led to the development of Critical Management Studies, which seeks to challenge this conception by deliberately taking sides with those who are adversely affected by the exercise of power through management (Alvesson et al., 2009).

But Becker's question does not necessarily involve taking sides either with management, or with those oppressed by these powerful social forces. Neither does it preclude the possibility of research being radical in its effects, since by questioning the taken for granted and the status quo, management research can sometimes threaten and destabilise established power interests. This is what some people have taken Becker to mean when he asked researchers to consider whose side they were on. Instead of suggesting that an objective stance in research is impossible, some see Becker's point as being that objectivity is difficult to achieve in practice (Hammersley, 2001). Political and methodological objectivity is therefore seen as something that ought to be strived for, by avoiding the development of sympathies that compromise the standards of good scientific work and what Becker called 'sentimentality', a condition that causes us to look away from something that we would prefer not to acknowledge. The importance of systematic, scientific research techniques therefore lies in their ability to be used in a way which forces us to challenge our commonly held assumptions about the phenomenon we are studying.

Wray-Bliss (2003) has written provocatively about the issue of taking sides in management research, arguing that researchers have a tendency to assume a position of superiority in relation to the people they study. This, he argues, applies to critical as well as mainstream management studies, despite its ambitions to represent or 'give voice' to those who are disadvantaged and oppressed by managerial interests. His analysis focuses on how research is written, and the ways that researchers present research participants as unable to effectively resist managerial oppression. This reinforces the authority of researchers 'who can position themselves as knowing better' (Wray-Bliss, 2003: 318) than their research participants. He concludes that we need to reflect on how power relations in the research process affect both the researched and the researcher, each of whom exercises power over the other.

It is not difficult to find instances where these kinds of power-laden assumptions about the superior judgement of the researcher are written into published research articles; this includes the tendency to refer to people being studied as 'research subjects', and to use theoretical language that they would be unlikely to understand. Even in considerations of research ethics, the assumption that those who are studied need to be protected from harm (by for example anonymising data so that the person cannot be identified), is somewhat presumptuous and potentially patronising, since they may not wish to be treated in this way (Bell and Bryman, 2007).

Dangerous liaisons

So exactly how do management researchers' assumptions, interactions and interpretations influence the research process? A classic example which is routinely cited as illustrative of this is the Hawthorne studies, mentioned earlier in relation to the importance of maintaining flexibility and the possibility of adapting your research design part-way through a study. The Hawthorne studies are interesting for the way that research participants, in this case a group of women assembly line workers, responded to the introduction of changes in their work environment and to the presence of a researcher in the room, who was instructed to observe but not to interact with them conversationally. The conclusion that the researchers eventually reached was that the very fact of participating in an experimental study had altered the women's behaviour.

But there are a couple of problems in generalising from this example. The first relates to the obvious power relations between the research team, who were mainly male and included several Harvard Business School professors, and the research participants – women manual workers, referred to as 'girls' in the published study (Roethlisberger and Dickson, 1939). The extent to which the young, immigrant women workers in the study responded positively to the changes is likely to have been affected by the power relations between them and the male researchers and supervisors. There is also evidence to suggest that the researchers treated the women workers in the studies very differently from male workers (Acker and Van Houten, 1974). And this is potentially misleading because it gives the impression that research participants seek to cooperate with or even to please researchers, which is often not the case in management research, particularly when studying elite groups, including business leaders and management consultants. These groups may have an active interest in not exposing their practices to external scrutiny by allowing them to be studied, especially if they think that this is likely to call them into question and thereby threaten the dominant power structure. Secondly, the Hawthorne studies provide little insight into the complex interactional processes whereby traditional scientific researcher/research participant relationships are undermined and alternatives are formed. This is understandable. The research was done in the 1920s and 1930s, well before alternatives to this model in the form of interpretive and other postpositivist research traditions had become better established. The example is therefore limited in its ability to prepare management researchers for the complexities of forming and maintaining contemporary research relationships.

Instead we will use a film to draw attention to the embodied, emotional and power laden aspects of management research relationships. Film can provide a naturalistic substitute for direct experience, thereby providing a safer way of learning about the research process (Saldaña, 2008). *Kitchen Stories* (2003) is a delightfully idiosyncratic and gently humorous Norwegian film set in the 1950s which tells the story of what happens when a group of researchers set out to study people's domestic habits. The film begins as the Swedish Home Research Institute, having already created the perfect kitchen for the national housewife, sets its sights on observing the habits of Norwegian bachelors. A number of bachelors have volunteered to participate in the study on the promise of an incentive, in the form of a horse (which turns out not to be a real horse, as the bachelor-volunteer in our story expected, but a decorative wooden one). The team of researchers is assembled for a formal briefing. Their role is to act as 'inspectors' in the home of the volunteer by sitting on a chair at the top of a raised platform in the volunteer's kitchen and recording all movement and activity that takes place in the room in a notebook for several weeks. The researchers are told that under no circumstances must they speak to or otherwise interact with the research subjects. To make the possibility of interaction between them less likely, each researcher is given a small caravan which they park next to the bachelor's house and live in for the duration of the study.

Through a series of gradually unfolding scenes, the somewhat bizarre scientific relationship between the researcher and the researched is first depicted, and then subverted. Initially, the researcher follows the rules set by the Swedish Home Research Institute to the letter, causing the bachelor to feel resentful and to avoid spending time in his kitchen. But when the bachelor offers the researcher a cup of coffee and some tobacco, the researcher eventually accepts these small gestures of friendship. At the beginning, the focus is on the actions of the bachelor, as the closely observed research subject. But as the film progresses, a shift in the balance of power takes place, when the bachelor makes a hole in the ceiling through which he is able to secretly observe his observer. Living in a relatively isolated rural situation, the researcher and the research subject overcome their mutual isolation and become increasingly friendly with one another, to the point where, one night, they get drunk together. The tables are turned completely when the researcher, recovering from a hangover, is confined to bed and the bachelor assumes the researcher's observation point on the raised chair, from where he records his own patterns of movement in the researcher's notebook. Not unsurprisingly, these activities are not looked upon favourably by the Swedish Home Research Institute and the researcher eventually loses his job.

You are probably thinking that such a research design as this film portrays is far-fetched and ludicrous, the stuff of fiction. Yet the film is loosely based on a programme of research conducted at Cornell University in the United States, informed by ideas of efficiency and based on the application of principles of scientific management. Through the study of kitchen 'workers', the research identified the ideal kitchen layout as comprised of a triangle of appliances and workspaces that minimised the amount of time spent moving around the space (Beyer, 1953). So *Kitchen Stories* is essentially a story based on a study of management.

This is significant, because it enables a pervasive feature of management research to be highlighted, namely the tendency to develop methods of study that assume the management researcher and the people they study are rational actors, and to therefore try to minimise any non-rational, or emotional interaction between them. This feature of management research is also something we see in the practice of management. Hence the norms of research are shaped by the field of study that it focuses upon. The film also draws attention to the tensions involved in researching forms of practice, such as people's domestic or working habits, where it is almost impossible to avoid influencing the object of study. It also shows that study is a two-way process, 'while the researcher attends to the study of other persons and their activities, these other persons attend to the study of the researcher and his/her activities' (Van Maanen and Kolb, 1985: 6). Finally, it raises the possibility that trying to avoid or eliminate interactions between the researcher and the researched may be counterproductive, resulting in the production of less meaningful data.

Inquiry from the inside

Some management researchers try to deal with these issues by seeking 'respondent validation', involving research subjects or participants[1] in the research process and consulting with them to find out whether findings make sense to them (see Marshall, 1995). Other management researchers go a step further, developing collaborative, participatory or action research strategies, where the subject of study is defined in conjunction with research participants. Two methodologies in particular have become popular, one on either side of the Atlantic. The North American variant is labelled 'appreciative inquiry', and was developed by Cooperrider and colleagues (Cooperrider and Srivastva, 1987) at the Case Western Reserve University. The European variant is called 'action research', and was developed by UK-based researchers, Eden and Huxham (1996), among others. Both approaches became popular in the 1980s, although action research can be traced back to the work of Lewin (1951), mentioned earlier. Although there are important differences between them, the primary feature that unifies them is that inquiry is seen as something that needs to be conducted from the inside, with the involvement of non-researchers in the research process, to understand the particularities of a given situation. Evered and Louis (1981) contrast this with 'inquiry from the outside', which calls for the researcher to remain detached from the situation that they are studying, as advocated by the Swedish Home Research Institute in *Kitchen Stories*.

This type of research is oriented towards solving a practical problem that participants face in their everyday lives. In this type of study some members of the organisation being studied are actively involved in negotiating the process and outcomes of the research and influencing the research findings. This directly contradicts positivist research which assumes that the goal of research is the production of knowledge that is unmediated and unaffected by the process of study. If researchers at the Swedish Home Research Institute featured in *Kitchen Stories* had started by asking the Norwegian bachelor what problems he faced in his everyday life, we might reasonably surmise that he would not have spoken about his need for a more efficiently designed kitchen workspace. Instead he might have spoken about his need for friendship to counter feelings of isolation and loneliness. Hence, as Bartunek (1993) observes, useful organisational knowledge rarely arises as a consequence of positivistic inquiry conducted from the outside. Crucially, close engagement with practice through action research can enable management researchers not only to gain better understanding of practice, but also potentially to change practice through intervention.

Of course, being intimately involved in practice, while simultaneously trying to study it, brings its own problems. Such problems are well known as a particular feature of participant observation, a research and data collection technique closely associated with ethnographic styles of research. Participant observation is a disciplined method through which the researcher alternates between an insider (participant) and an outsider (observer) position. By moving between these two stances the researcher is able to engage in inquiry from the inside, while also maintaining a degree of scientific objectivity in relation to the object of study. This analytical stance is also associated with the idea of the 'professional stranger' (Simmel, 1950), which reflects the inherent contradictions involved in maintaining distance and proximity in a research situation simultaneously.

While participant observation is particularly associated with organisational ethnography, we think that it applies much more widely within management research as a practice-based form of inquiry. This includes what Brannick and Coghlan (2007) define as 'insider research', studies where the person doing the research is also an organisational member. Insider research, as writers like Brannick and Coghlan note, brings with it certain advantages, such as greater opportunities for access and the prior understanding that the researcher has in relation to the setting, as well as some disadvantages, for instance in making the difficulties in maintaining role duality even greater.

Much ethnographic storytelling in management, as well as in other disciplines, has therefore traditionally been devoted to telling heroic, romantic tales about negotiating the 'thorny mazeway' (Van Maanen and Kolb, 1985) that separates insiders from outsiders. A typical example is given by Lupton (1985) who describes his 'social anthropological method' as being 'simply to take a job as a worker, openly declare myself to everyone as an investigator and then lose myself in the work group'. This realist narrative tale (Van Maanen, 1988) presents the researcher as a dispassionate experiential authority who is able to immerse himself in the setting in order to achieve interpretive omnipotence.

Some ethnographic accounts also detail the perils of 'going native', as the condition wherein this duality is lost. The researcher consequently loses the ability to critically analyse the situation they are studying through having identified too closely with research participants, or 'taking sides' with them. This is associated with what Denzin and Lincoln (2005) label the 'traditional period' of qualitative research when ethnography was associated with acts of colonial domination and conquest (Prasad, 2005). It leads to what Van Maanen (1988) calls 'confessional tales', wherein the researcher provides an account of their ordeal of fieldwork and how they overcame various obstacles. Although writers such as Denzin and Lincoln see the traditional period of qualitative research as a moment confined to the early 1900s, these conventions and the classic anthropological studies that illustrate them, remain popular in organisational ethnography (see Neyland, 2008, for example). This encourages an authoritative style of analysis that positions the researcher in superior relation to research participants.

And yet practice-oriented approaches to management research such as those described here are relatively uncommon, and the vast majority of management research is based on inquiry from an outsider perspective. Even 'experience-near' (Geertz, 1974) research methods like ethnography, which have a long tradition in management research, are not being practised as much as they used to be (Zickar and Carter, 2010), leading some to suggest that management researchers have become superficial in their engagement with practice, embarking on 'jet plane' excursions into the field that are so brief researchers rarely need to take a toothbrush with them (Bate, 1997). This compromises the underlying logic of ethnography which relies on achieving a degree of insider status through building trust with research subjects through a lengthy period of engagement. The reasons for the relative paucity of practice-oriented, experience-near studies of management are complex and some of them we have already discussed but suffice to say there is still a degree of suspicion surrounding this kind of research and a tendency to assume that by involving research subjects in a study, the researcher risks undermining the perceived scientific neutrality and objectivity of their investigation.

Through a glass darkly: practising reflection and reflexivity

So how can management researchers respond to the question of who they are and how this shapes their approach to research? Michael Agar (2008) suggests researchers should start by deliberately cultivating awareness, or reflecting on these issues. He frames this by posing the question, 'who are you to do this?' The point of such reflection is not to determine whether or not the researcher is biased, but instead to understand what kinds of personal and cultural biases exist, how they shape the process of research, and to find ways of documenting their influence. Practising reflection is not simply a matter of the researcher noting any personal identity characteristics that they consider salient (e.g. being a white, heterosexual male), which potentially could have influenced the research, and then moving (swiftly) on. Instead, reflection implies a deliberate ongoing commitment to seeing self and identity as central to the process of research and considering how this shapes the conclusions drawn from the analysis (Coffey, 1999). It is an ingrained habit (Holland, 1999) that involves alternating between reflecting on the process of research, and actually doing it, perhaps by having an internal conversation with yourself (Archer, 2003). The result is greater self-understanding about your own position, which is used to inform the knowledge that is generated.

Yet as implied by the phrase 'through a glass darkly', any attempt to account for how our identities as researchers influence the research process can only ever be partial and speculative because any alternatives can only be considered counterfactually, as something that may potentially have influenced the research process, but whose actual influence cannot be known. During her PhD research (carried out in male-dominated organisations where she was often the only woman present), Emma had cause to reflect on how her gender was influencing fieldwork relationships and how the data she collected might have been different if the research was done by a man. She read several ethnographic accounts written by male organisational ethnographers which implied that the close social relations enabled by the researcher and research subjects' shared masculinities enabled the generation of more credible and trustworthy insider accounts. But the point of practising reflection is not to determine which subject position is 'best' in relation to particular research settings. Instead it assumes that all research involves subject relations that shape the knowledge created. The task therefore is to take account of them in a way which is ethically and analytically productive (Bell, 1999).

Ideas about management research as a process of reflection are complicated by the closely related notion of reflexivity. A distinction is often made between reflection, the process of observing how we do research (as implied by the idea of holding up a mirror to ourselves and looking into it), and reflexivity, a process of self-reflection based on questioning how research is done (Hibbert et al., 2010). Reflexivity involves the researcher asking, 'what are my assumptions; what am I taking for granted in this context?' But the distinction between reflection and reflexivity is not at all watertight.

The popularity of reflexivity in management research is connected to with the influence of postmodernism and the crisis of representation which, beginning in the 1990s, called into question the possibility of building objective notions of truth through scientific study. It is thus associated with unsettling 'distinctions we make between what is fact or fiction, the nature of knowledge, and ultimately our purpose and practice as researchers' (Cunliffe, 2003: 985). Such arguments imply that we may never come to understand or represent another person's 'worldview' through research. Taken to its logical conclusion, reflexivity calls into question what can really be known through management research, by challenging the idea that research data can provide an accurate representation of reality.

Reflexivity is also seen as something that can be practised in the moment of research, what Weick (2002) calls 'real-time reflexivity', as well as afterwards. Riach (2009) talks about the importance of 'sticky moments' in developing reflexivity: when the research protocol or context is actively questioned by participants or breaks down. Through raising questions about her age and her reasons for being interested in the research topic of age inequality, sticky moments caused Riach to question her own expectations and preconceptions about the research interaction. Reflexive accounts such as Riach's (2009) also draw attention to the suspicion that participants may feel about a researcher's motives for doing a study, seeing it as a self-interested way for someone to build a career by gaining a qualification (in her case a PhD). This is not unusual. As Buchanan et al. (1988) suggest, management researchers are often, and perhaps rightly, seen as primarily concerned with getting in to an organisation, getting the data, and getting out again so that they can write it up. Reflexivity can enable these uncomfortable truths to be explored, perhaps with the aim of developing greater reciprocity, through which research of mutual benefit to researcher and participants can be developed (Bell and Bryman, 2007).

A great deal of theoretical attention has been devoted to categorising different types and constructing various models of reflexivity in management research. For example, Johnson and Duberley (2003) distinguish between three different kinds of reflexivity. Methodological reflexivity is, they say, associated with positivist research and involves monitoring how research is affected by the presence and actions of the researcher, such as those identified in the Hawthorne studies. Deconstructive reflexivity is more closely associated with interpretive research and involves the researcher questioning their own methodological and theoretical assumptions and trying to understand how research participants see their situation. Epistemic reflexivity could be seen as the basis for practice-oriented forms of research mentioned earlier, since it involves seeking out collaborative research relationships as the basis for knowledge creation. Similarly, Alvesson et al. (2008) focus on the implications for research writing that reflexivity raises, arguing that there are distinct sets of practices that arise from reflexivity that relate to the representation of multiple perspectives. The reflexive process can, they say, give voice to a less powerful 'Other', enable recognition of 'positioning practices' involved in knowledge creation, destabilising positivist versions of knowledge production. In a related vein, Cunliffe (2002) sees reflexivity as a radical, dialogical enterprise, in which researchers must analyse their own ways of speaking and writing in order to understand how knowledge is created through language. Using the metaphor of 'social poetics', she emphasises the embodied and relational nature of management knowledge production as constructed through metaphor and storytelling. Given the fundamental ontological questioning entailed in the reflexive project, it is perhaps unsurprising that reflexivity has been described as a meta-process that affects 'the whole way of life of reflexive researchers' (Hibbert et al., 2010: 48). In short, it seems that reflexivity has become 'a word with which to conjure' (Brannick and Coghlan, 2006: 143) in management research.

And yet despite this elaborate theorising, there is remarkably little published management research in which reflexivity, or even reflection, appears to be practised to any significant extent. In fact, some of the most extensively reflexive research in organisational contexts has been done outside the management research field, such as by Kondo (1990), a cultural anthropologist, whose ethnographic account of her own experience on the shop floor of a Tokyo factory exposes the identity work involved in being a Japanese–American woman who through the course of the fieldwork, acquired culturally meaningful Japanese roles in order to become immersed in the culture. The few reflexive analyses that do exist in management research tend to be confined to particular kinds of qualitative research, such as auto-ethnography, where the researcher uses their own personalised experiences as the basis for analysing and writing about a culture (Humphries, 2005; Bell and King, 2010). The vast majority of published accounts of the management research process such as those in journal articles, contain very little in the way of reflexive analysis of the researcher's own identity that would enable the reader to assess who they were to do this. Instead researchers focus almost exclusively on technical issues relating to how the data was collected and analysed, and the researcher's identity is written out of the text. Hence it seems that management researchers are not required to 'bare their souls, only their procedures' (Lofland and Lofland, 1995: 13).

A number of writers have suggested that the lack of reflexive writing in management research is a reflection of the career risks associated with exposing one's professional practice in this way, especially for junior researchers, women and people of colour (Parry and Boyle, 2009). Consequently, it is much more common for the language of the distanced, external observer to be used in management research, indicated by third person tropes such as 'it is the view of this author', rather than first person statements, because the former reinforces the idea of objectivist researcher as dispassionately interested in their subject of study. Hatch (1996) argues that the objectivist mode of researcher self-presentation, whether externally or self-imposed, can cause them to become alienated from their research through the development of an 'ill-fitted research identity' (Hatch, 1996: 368).

She also suggests that the relationship between doing research and writing about it is mutually constitutive, so the decision to assume the narrative position of the distanced observer in writing is likely to subtly shape the entire research process, including earlier stages of data collection and analysis in a way which undermines the development of closer research-practice relationships. Yet even if you do not declare who you are in your writing, sometimes other researchers who read your work will do this for you. Brewis (2005) writes about this in relation to her study of sex work, arguing that a particular sexuality and sexual relations were inscribed upon her through other researchers' readings of her work, as they sought to interpret why she was interested in this subject. This example draws attention to the way in which the subject of study and the identity of the researcher can be conflated by research audiences.

Overall, reflexivity in management research seem to be a minority sport that is talked about in abstract terms much more frequently than it is actually practiced. Could this be because through all the talk of profound uncertainty, fallibility and the impossibility of knowing, the term has become paralyzing, and has deterred all but the most intellectually adept, philosophically-oriented management researchers from engaging with it? Weick (2002) argues that by constructing the 'self-as-theorist' we have become far too reflexive, indulgently engaging in pointless debates about the value of the knowledge that we create and the role of the researcher in its creation, rather than simply finding out about other people and the organizations in which they operate. Writers like Weick advocate the practice of 'instrumental reflexivity', wherein one limits the extent of reflection so as to enable ongoing practice.

It is important that reflexivity is not seen as the sole preserve of a relatively small group of postmodern or qualitatively oriented management researchers. Holland (1999: 476) says that reflexivity is 'the best criterion of a truly human science'. It is unfortunate that many management researchers seem to be deterred from engaging with these ideas, or are able to dismiss them as 'postmodern' and therefore largely irrelevant to traditional, mainstream management research. Perhaps management research is a field in which scholars and practitioners yearn for certainty and are therefore less likely to practise self-awareness or engage in reflexivity because this highlights the inevitable partiality of knowledge claims. And yet reflection has long been seen as fundamental to management, as a complement to action and an important means of learning through practice (Schön, 1983). Reflective learning processes are also seen as fundamental to the development of successful communities of practice (Lave and Wenger,

1991). Learning through reflecting on action is therefore a fundamental aspect of being a management researcher.

Feelings and bodies in the field

The trend towards reflexivity also implies that attention should be paid to the role of emotions in shaping the research process and the accounts that this produces (Brannan, 2011). Our experience of doing research and talking to others suggests this is an issue that is rarely spoken about in formal methods training. Instead it seems that 'there remains something of a silence surrounding *researchers'* own emotional experiences' (Kenny, 2008: 376, emphasis in original). From the frustration and disappointment that arises when a protracted and difficult access negotiation falls through, or when an interviewee refuses to answer the questions that the researcher puts to him, to the feelings of excitement and pleasure that arise when a fascinating document is discovered in the company archive, or the results of a questionnaire survey generate some surprising findings, doing management research is an emotional process. Hence it is hard to disagree with Brannan (2011) when he says that management research is an 'emotionally intensive' activity.

Reflexivity also invites us to think about the embodied nature of research activity, whether this involves taking a job in a company as a way of gaining research access, or presenting research findings to research participants or other researchers at conferences. Again, it is experience-near management researchers, like organisational ethnographers, who have been most willing to write about these aspects of the research process. For example, Kenny (2008) describes her alternation between feelings of belonging, including warmth and solidarity, which were contrasted with periods of emotional exclusion, hurt and abjection in the course of her ethnographic study of a development organisation.

Acknowledging emotion and embodied experience is thus a crucial aspect of reflexive practice in management research. The reason this has been largely overlooked is suggested to relate to cultural definitions of research as a rational-objectivist and masculine activity (Brannan, 2011). There are some signs that emotionality and embodiment are becoming more widely accepted as an aspect of reflexive practice, particularly among qualitative management researchers. The challenge is for emotion and embodiment not to be seen as inherently compromising the neutrality and objectivity of management research, and therefore as things to be hidden and avoided. Instead, ethical reflexivity in management research involves acknowledging and working with these aspects of human social experience in a way which recognises their unavoidability and seeks to work constructively with them.

And so to ethics

Recently, Emma was teaching a research methods course to a group of postgraduate management research students, when she bumped into one of them in the corridor. 'Sorry I didn't make it to last week's session' he said, 'It was on ethics wasn't it?' Emma nodded. 'That's ok then', replied the student, 'because I've already completed my ethical approval form and had it signed off by my supervisor'. It is not hard to see what's wrong with this situation, as ethics, which includes assumptions about what is morally right and wrong in management research, appears to have been defined as marginal to the research process. Hence it is something that the student sees as arising at a particular moment, usually during the planning stage, when it is considered and dealt with, and then set to one side. What is more difficult to ascertain is how such a situation arises, and what might be done to redress it.

Growing attention has been devoted to research ethics in the social sciences in recent years, partly as a consequence of the rise of 'oversight regimes', including university research ethics committees which formally monitor ethical practice in research carried out under the auspices of the university (Bell and Bryman, 2007). This has resulted in the generation of a number of clearly and consistently defined precepts (covering avoidance of harm and deception, informed consent, privacy, confidentiality and anonymity), that are applied very consistently across the social sciences. You can easily find out more about these precepts by looking up on the internet any one of the research ethics codes produced by associations that represent social science researchers, such as the *American Psychological Association*, the *Social Research Association* or the *Academy of Management*. Most of this guidance focuses on relationships with research subjects. But questions about what is right and wrong in management research are much broader than this potentially implies, covering issues relating to researcher misconduct, including falsification and fabrication of data and plagiarism. The pressures on management researchers to 'publish or perish' have made the need to consider ethical issues in a more encompassing way by extending the focus beyond research subjects.

You might think that such a high degree of clarity and consistency about what is morally justifiable in research is a sign that ethical standards in management research are high and consistently applied. However, one issue of concern is that ethical formalism and audit cultures have in some cases resulted in a compliance orientation towards ethics in management research which (as the example used to introduce this section illustrates), can lead to the abdication of ethical agency and responsibility in favour of rule-following conformity. This is sometimes called the 'tick box' approach to research ethics (Bell and Wray-Bliss, 2009). This can encourage a focus on minimal standards, applied to certain kinds of research, rather than seeing ethics as an ongoing consideration that is central to the conduct of all research. Added to this, there are concerns that the bureaucratisation of ethics constitutes a threat to the conduct of certain kinds of management research, particularly inductive studies involving action research and ethnography, where for example it is not possible in advance of a study for a researcher to know exactly who will be involved and therefore who they need to obtain informed consent from.

This has led some management researchers to be dismissive of ethical oversight mechanisms, seeing them as an impediment to researcher freedom. Our view is more pragmatic; while we don't see them as offering universal solutions to complex ethical tensions in the research process, and we are opposed to the notion that there is a single ethical standard that all management researchers should apply, we do think that concerns about ethics in management research can be used to prompt consideration of how researchers ought to be, rather than focused on monitoring what they do. Such an approach is aspirational, rather than oriented towards compliance (Bell and Wray-Bliss, 2009). The dangers of not considering ethics are highlighted repeatedly in business, where the existence of ethical rules and regulations provides no guarantee of ethical behaviour, as the 2001 Enron scandal highlighted (copies of the company's 65 page *Code of Ethical Conduct* were reportedly sold on e-bay as an ironic memento). As countless analyses of business ethics also highlight, ethical action relies on cultural enactment in addition to bureaucratic structure, a point which equally applies to management research as well as management practice.

The most important point however, is that research ethics cannot be divorced from professional or personal ethics. If a technical instrumental approach is taken to management research that is focused on employing the most rationally efficient methods to achieve a goal, then moral issues concerning the processes through which it is achieved and the purposes to which research is put are unlikely to be considered. Ethics therefore need to be at the heart of management research, shaping our relationships within the community as well as those who constitute the focus of our research.

Conclusion

In this chapter we have explored how issues relating to identity and ethics fundamentally shape the management research process. We have argued that these considerations are not optional but central to all types of management research, rather than being relevant to specific kinds of study which involve forming relationships with research participants. But the arguments in this chapter go deeper than this. For it is through partitioning issues of reflexivity and ethics that the technical-rational approach to management research that we have been critical of throughout this book, has been allowed to dominate. Hence we need to think about the values that inform our community and our individual research practice, and to position ethical and identity related concerns as legitimate, rather than something to be concealed in authorised accounts of the management research process.

Note

1   The question of whether to use the term research 'subjects' or 'participants' has already been raised. The latter term is more common in postpositivist research, or where a participative element is involved in the study.

Conclusion

What Kind of Management Researcher Are You?

> There is a widespread notion that science has become a problem in calculation, fabricated in laboratories or statistical filing systems just as 'in a factory,' a calculation involving only the cool intellect and not one's 'heart and soul.' (Max Weber, 1918/2009: 135)

> Many students have found that field work is an excellent opportunity to get off campus. (James P. Spradley and David W. McCurdy, 1972: 4)

The choices about management research philosophy, theory, methodology and methods explained in this short book will inevitably be shaped by the kind of person you are and the beliefs and values that you hold. For example, if you are someone who is happiest working alone studying old documents in the dusty basement of a library, or enjoys sitting in front of a PC monitor manipulating statistical data, you are unlikely to be comfortable doing a collaborative action research project that involves working closely with managers of an organisation to address their problems. Similarly, if you see yourself as a champion of minority group interests in the face of managerial exploitation, there is little sense in you pursuing research questions that focus on improving managerial efficiency as an assumed good.

The point is that these researcher identities are not necessarily better or worse, each has something to offer, and this diversity has the potential to enrich and enhance the community of management research as a whole. The point too is that management research is primarily a means of generating meaningful, and hopefully in some sense useful knowledge, and any systematic technique through which this can potentially be achieved should be embraced. But we are not saying that 'anything goes' in management research. We have been critical in this book of the kind of relativistic researcher positioning which involves selecting methods or philosophies that are assumed to be the most legitimate by funding bodies, or elite journals that the researcher wishes to target. This highly pragmatic approach towards management research encourages an instrumental, game-playing attitude that is detrimental to the long term future of the field.

Management research is a practice that is learnt by doing. It is, to borrow from Feyerabend (1993: 157), more 'sloppy' and 'irrational' than most methodological accounts in conventional textbooks or published research articles would lead us to believe. For writers like Feyerabend, the principles of methodological positivism are an inaccurate representation of how scientific research really works. And by trying to make management research appear ever more rational and precise, we are in danger of losing what makes it interesting and worthwhile as a practice in the first place. For as Feyerabend reminds us, without chaos, there is no knowledge. But this does not preclude reflecting on the process of doing research, in the way we have tried to do in this book. Management researchers may only come to understand their methods after they have done their research. *Post hoc* reflection can help to dispel the mystique that can surround the research process, and in so doing can open up spaces for greater flexibility and innovation in future research practice.

At this point you might be asking, 'what do I make of this book? Ought I to take the claims of Bell and Thorpe seriously? Should what they say in any way affect how I think about or do management research, or should I just continue in the same way as before? It's all very well for them', you may say, 'they hold a position of relative job security within management research, from which they can afford to question the practices of the community without this adversely affecting their careers or their professional status. And besides, if the ideas in this book are dismissed by the management research community, they always have their conventional research methods textbooks to fall back on!'

You would be entirely justified in making these points. Our intention in this short book is therefore not to try to win the argument or impose our views on you. In seeking to practice the kind of reflexivity we have preached, we know that it is impossible for us to speak about these issues without drawing on our personal experiences and promoting our own interests. The way we see management research is inevitably shaped by our methodological, philosophical and theoretical beliefs and values. Added to this, there is a risk that by writing this book we are trying 'to salve our consciences through revealing our awareness of the disciplinary practices in which we participate' (Bell and King, 2010: 11). However we hope that our desire to make the purpose and process of management research more explicit is motivated by more than this. In what follows we offer a few final thoughts, which we hope might form the basis for ongoing community-based conversations about what management research is and why we do it.

Making time for management research

Weber's speech on science as a vocation, given at Munich University in 1918, is a good place to start in contemplating the time pressures associated with management research. Weber uses the term 'vocation' to describe the attitude of contemporary social scientists. This involves combining professionalism with a more esoteric sensibility which is similar to the religious notion of a calling to God. Weber sees vocation as carrying connotations of sacrifice based on the command of God. This relies on the individual freely giving themselves to the task to which they are called. Yet in his essay he also tries to expose the idealistic temptation

> … to focus on the inner vocation for science rather than on its external conditions… by demonstrating the potentially tragic consequences of failing to acknowledge the real conditions of scientific work in the modern university. (Owen and Strong, 2004: xxv).

What are the implications of Weber's argument for management research? It is quite common for management research communities to draw on the concept of inner vocation to explain why and how they do research. Let us give you some examples. One of the first management research conferences that Emma attended in Finland (shortly after finishing her PhD and having left her two children to be cared for by her partner), opened with a Sunday afternoon plenary at which a famous female professor claimed that the high attendance in the room suggested that management researchers see themselves as pursuing a vocation.

Our second example is based on an introductory article from the editor in the *Academy of Management Journal,* which states that the culture of management professors is defined by a 'commitment to a calling'. The (female) author of the article defines a calling as accepting the norms of a career wherein professional work is never regarded only as a means to an end but as an end in itself. She goes on to say 'I can attest that for some of us, the commitment to the calling can erase the lines between work and leisure hours almost entirely!' (Hillman, 2005: 186). Our third example concerns an email which Emma received from a journal editor in response to her submission of a research article for consideration. The email was dated Sunday 11.29am and began 'Emma – I read your paper yesterday and have some feedback'. Management researchers thus utilise the concept of inner vocation in a way which has connotations of sacrifice based on total, passionate commitment, 24/7.

These practices blur the boundaries of research, so that there is little boundary between time spent on research and time used in other ways. As any management researcher will tell you, one of the hardest aspects of management research is to plan and manage your time, since there is little structure imposed by your supervisor or your employer, except in the form of measuring research outputs such as the dissertation or a research paper. This requires a good deal of self discipline, not just for full-time management researchers planning a university-based academic career, but also for part-time researchers, such as Masters students who may have to complete a research project in a very short time period, or be expected to juggle the demands of a paid job and family alongside their research. The resultant tendency is towards the temporal 'ever-availability' (Zerubavel, 1981), or complete social accessibility of the management researcher, wherever she or he is located.

These examples illustrate a socialisation process which prescribes behaviour through the adoption of certain values about the central place of research work in life. These powerful cultural norms established by management research communities encourage members to self manage and make sacrifices in order to be a successful management researcher. Research work is defined as an identity project that consumes the entire self through its requirement for passionate pursuit, irrespective of the external conditions within which this pursuit is located. Rarely is there any apparent reflection on the ethics associated with this self-disciplinary orientation. As a form of cultural control it relies on self-management practised by a community that does not appear to show much sign of thinking there is anything that needs to be questioned about these practices, which tend to disproportionately disadvantage those who have caring commitments (often women), or limited resources, for example to attend international conferences. These cultural norms are typically communicated hierarchically by more experienced researchers, like journal editors for example, who are highly influential in shaping the values and practices of the management research community. It also highlights the differences between members of the management research community in terms of their agency and capacity to challenge these normative practices.

Unlike in Weber's analysis, the conception of vocation upon which these practices are based largely fails to acknowledge the external conditions of research work in the modern university, the pressures of which have increased considerably since the early 1900s, when Weber was writing. The 'publish or perish' mentality, which we have critiqued in this book, has changed the career profile of a management researcher in important ways, and this has worrying implications for the future diversity of the management research community.

▬▬▬ Other ways of knowing

Management research is relatively conservative in defining what constitutes legitimate knowledge and the methods that should be used to generate it. Consequently, it has been relatively slow to pick up on trends currently affecting other social scientific disciplines which call for the development of alternative modes of inquiry to capture and represent the social world that we inhabit and seek to understand. This has given rise to methods that seek to capture embodied, affective and emotional aspects of knowing, by drawing on traditions that go beyond the ideas of rigour, rationality and empiricism which form the basis of traditional scientific inquiry. It includes methods of visual analysis, as well as approaches that draw on performance in order to try to access prediscursive forms of knowing that are acquired through experience. It is somewhat ironic that management consultants and market researchers have been more imaginative and willing to experiment with these 'soft' methods, and the philosophies that inform them, than management researchers themselves (Law, 2004). There are some indications that this attitude may be gradually changing. For example, Emma is involved in the *in*Visio research network (International Network for Visual Studies in Organisations, www.in-visio.org), founded in 2008 to develop shared practice among visual management researchers.

As others observe (Law, 2004), there is a high degree of cultural and historical specificity associated with the designation of certain research methods as legitimate and others not. Management research has traditionally been dominated by concepts, models and theories that originate in the Anglo-Saxon world. As the management research community becomes more internationally diverse, there are opportunities to challenge these Euro–American assumptions, by doing research that not only spans more diverse empirical contexts, such as China, Brazil, the Middle East, India and the continent of Africa (where the first Academy of Management Africa Conference was held in 2013), but also draws on different epistemological traditions of knowledge creation. This relies on retaining a methodologically pluralistic approach to management research, and resisting some of the pressures towards conformity and uniformity talked about in this book.

Yanow and Schwartz-Shea's (2006) concept of humanistic science is helpful here. Management research is indisputably a human, rather than a natural science, since it is concerned with the social rather than the natural world. Their use of the term humanistic science draws attention to the ethics of research, characterised by whether researchers are willing to 'apply their own theories and research findings to themselves' (2006: 389). This relates to ideas about reflexivity, discussed in the previous chapter, and invites consideration of the power and politics of management research through posing the question 'knowledge for whom?' Humanistic science also encourages us to pursue local knowledge based on human connection, by getting out and seeking to understand the diversity of management practice. This, as in the quote from Weber with which we introduced this conclusion, is a battle for the heart and soul of research, against the forces of what Yanow and Schwartz-Shea (2006: 391) call 'depersonalizing technicism and depersonalized rationalism'.

Communities of purpose

Throughout this book we have drawn upon the notion of communities as a way of understanding how management research is organised. Communities of research practice are crucial in determining how the craft of management research is passed on to future generations. This can be a collective enterprise based on shared agreement about the norms and values of research that are being pursued. For example, doctoral researchers at Sobey School of Business at Saint Mary's University in Canada, spend time setting collective expectations in a way which seeks to develop a culture that encourages (rather than requires) research. Crucially, the emphasis is on research for a purpose. Students are encouraged to see research as about relevance, quality, rigour and fun. Here is an extract from their statement of research values:

- We need to be confident and proud but not arrogant.
- We need to be research active and not complacent.
- We need to continue to produce high level research but not just any research.
- We need to publish to push forward our ideas but not just for the sake of getting published.
- Success is often the outcome of several attempts.
- We need to be interested in what we are doing.
- We need to care about what we are doing.

You may notice that nowhere does this statement emphasise the status of the journal in which research is published. Nor does it preclude the possibility of disseminating research in other formats including books. Research students invariably ask questions relating to career choices at some point during their research studies and this provides opportunity for debates about publishing (can I get and keep a tenure track position without publishing in elite journals?) and ethics (how do I balance the pressure to publish with other pressures to develop a particular project of research?). What this highlights is the potential for social responsibility in management research, based on a broader purpose to try to influence if not change society, rather than as a self referential, career building activity. Research is done collaboratively and is seen above all as fun and purposeful. Sobey researchers are encouraged to continually remind themselves about the value of research as a way of contributing to change. Underlying this approach is the oft quoted aphorism of Karl Marx that 'philosophers may reflect on the world but the point is to change it'.

Conclusion

In 1972 James Spradley and David McCurdy wrote a book in which they advocated that research could be carried out by undergraduate students of anthropology. They argued that research encourages us to descend the ivory tower of the university and, as in the quote at the start of this chapter, to 'get off campus'. Research also enables us to enter into organisational settings where we might otherwise never go. They go on to say: 'It gives an excuse to visit local bars, churches, and prisons. It can be done at dog shows, hairdresser's shops, big-city newspaper offices, and at girl scout troop meetings. You may even ride with highway patrolmen or spend eight hours answering telephone calls at the police station' (Spradley and McCurdy, 1972: 4). They also observed that research fieldwork brought social science to life, enhancing understanding of theories and concepts through first-hand experience.

It was these kinds of sentiments which first got us interested in management research and continue to fascinate us today. A great deal has changed in the past few decades, in terms of the context within which management research is conducted and the issues that researchers have to consider. Added to this, the barriers to entry as a management researcher (for example in relation to publishing, or gaining research access), are probably higher. This may well deter some people from ever trying to do any original empirical research of the kind we have described in this book. Yet without research which enables theory to be connected to practice, it is hard to see how the knowledge upon which management as a field of practice and academic study can develop. We hope that this short book encourages you to take up this task and to enjoy it.

References

Abrahamson, E. (1991) 'Managerial fads and fashion: The diffusion and rejection of innovations', *Academy of Management Review*, 16: 586–612.

Acker, J. and Van Houten, D.R. (1974) 'Differential recruitment and control: The sex structuring of organizations', *Administrative Science Quarterly*, 19(2): 152–163.

Agar, M.H. (1980) *The Professional Stranger: An Informal Introduction to Ethnography*. San Diego: Academic Press.

Agar, M.H. (2008) *The Professional Stranger: An Informal Introduction to Ethnography*, 2nd edn. Bingley: Emerald.

Alvesson, M. (2003) 'Methodology for close up studies – struggling with closeness and closure', *Higher Education*, 46: 167–93.

Alvesson, M. and Kärreman, D. (2007) 'Creating mystery: Empirical matters in theory development', *Academy of Management Review*, 32(4): 1265–81.

Alvesson, M. and Sköldberg, K. (2000) *Reflexive Methodology: New Vistas for Qualitative Research*. London: Sage.

Alvesson, M., Hardy, C. and Harley, B. (2008) 'Reflecting on reflexivity: Reflexive textual practices in organization and management theory', *Journal of Management Studies*, 45(3): 480–501.

Alvesson, M., Bridgman, T. and Willmott, H. (2009) *The Oxford Handbook of Critical Management Studies*. Oxford: Oxford University Press.

Anderson, N., Heriot, G.P. and Hodgkinson, G. (2001) 'The practitioner researcher divide in industrial work and organizational psychology: Where are we now and where do we go from here?', *Journal of Occupational and Organizational Psychology*, 74: 391–411.

Archer, M. (1995) *Realist Social Theory: The Morphogenetic Approach*. Cambridge: Cambridge University Press.

Archer, M. (2003) *Structure, Agency and the Internal Conversation*. Cambridge: Cambridge University Press.

Bacharach, S.B. (1989) 'Organization Theories: Some criteria for evaluation', *Academy of Management Review*, 14(4): 496–515.

Barley, S. (2006) 'When I write my masterpiece: Thoughts on what makes a paper interesting', *Academy of Management Journal*, 49(1): 16–20.

Barthes, R. (1967) *Image, Music, Text*. London: Fontana Press.

Bartunek, J. (1993) 'Scholarly dialogues and participatory action research', *Human Relations*, 46(10): 1221–33.

Bartunek, J., Rynes, S.L. and Ireland, R.D. (2006) 'What makes management research interesting and why does it matter?' *Academy of Management Journal,* 49(1): 9–15.

Bate, S. (1997) 'Whatever happened to organizational ethnography? A review of the field of organizational ethnography and anthropological studies', *Human Relations,* 50(9): 1147–75.

Becher, T. (1989) *Academic Tribes and Territories: Intellectual Enquiry and the Cultures of Disciplines.* Buckingham: SRHE and Open University.

Becker, H.S. (1967) 'Whose side are we on?', *Social Problems,* 14: 239–47.

Bell, E. (1999) 'The negotiation of a working role in organizational ethnography', *International Journal of Social Research Methodology,* 2(1): 17–37.

Bell, E. (2011) 'Managerialism and management research: Would Melville Dalton get a job today?', in C. Cassell and B. Lee (eds), *Challenges and Controversies in Management Research.* London: Routledge. pp. 122–37.

Bell, E. and Bryman, A. (2007) 'The ethics of management research: An exploratory content analysis', *British Journal of Management,* 18(1): 63–77.

Bell, E. and King, D. (2010) 'The elephant in the room: Critical management studies conferences as a site of body pedagogics', *Management Learning,* 41(4): 429–42.

Bell, E. and Wray-Bliss, E. (2009) 'Research Ethics: Regulations and Responsibilities', in A. Bryman and D. Buchanan (eds), *Sage Handbook of Organizational Research Methods.* London: Sage. pp. 78–92.

Bennis, W. and O'Toole, J.O. (2005) 'How business schools lost their way', *Harvard Business Review,* 83(5): 98–104.

Berger, P. (2002) 'Whatever happened to sociology?', *First Things,* 126: 27–29.

Bergh, D. (2003) 'Thinking strategically about contribution', (editorial) *Academy of Management Journal,* 46(2): 135–6.

Beyer, G. (1953) *The Cornell Kitchen: Product Design through Research.* New York State College of Home Economics, in association with Cornell University Housing Research Center.

Bhaskar, R. (1978) *A Realist Theory of Science.* New York: Harvester Press.

Biglan, A. (1973) 'The characteristics of subject matter in different academic areas', *Journal of Applied Psychology,* 57(3): 195–203.

Boje, D. (1991) 'The storytelling organization: A study of performance in an office supply firm', *Administrative Science Quarterly,* 36: 106–26.

Boje, D. (2001) *Narrative Methods for Organizational and Communication Research.* London: Sage.

Booth, C. and Rowlinson, M. (2006) 'Management and organizational history: Prospects', *Management & Organizational History*, 1(1): 5–30.

Bourdieu, P. (1984) *Distinction*. London: Routledge.

Boyer, E. L. (1990) *Scholarship Reconsidered: Priorities of the Professoriate*, the Carnegie Foundation for the Advancement of Teaching, New York: Jossey-Bass.

Brannan, M. (2011) 'Researching emotions and the emotions of researching: The strange case of alexithymia in reflexive research', *International Journal of Work, Organisation and Emotion*, 4(3/4): 322–39.

Brannick, T. and Coghlan, D. (2006) 'Reflexivity in management and business research: What do we mean?', *Irish Journal of Management*, 27(2): 143–61.

Brannick, T. and Coghlan, D. (2007) 'In defense of being "native": The case for insider academic research', *Organizational Research Methods*, 10(1): 59–74.

Brewis, J. (2005) 'Signing my life away? Researching sex and organization', *Organization*, 12(4): 493–510.

Bryman, A. (2006) 'Paradigm peace and the implications for quality', *International Journal of Social Research Methodology*, 9(2): 111–26.

Buchanan, D. and Bryman, A. (2007) 'Contextualizing methods choice in organizational research', *Organizational Research Methods*, 10(3): 483–501.

Buchanan, D., Boddy, D. and McCalman, J. (1988) 'Getting in, getting out and getting back', in A. Bryman (ed.), *Doing Research in Organisations*. London: Routledge.

Burger, T. (1987) *Max Weber's Theory of Concept Formation: History, Laws and Ideal Types*. Durham: Duke University Press.

Burrell, G. (1996) 'Normal science, paradigms, metaphors, discourses and genealogies of analysis', in S. Clegg, C. Hardy and W.R. Nord (eds), *Handbook of Organization Studies*. London: Sage.

Burrell, G. (1997) *Pandemonium: Towards a Retro-Organization Theory*. London: Sage.

Burrell, G. and Morgan, G. (1979) *Sociological Paradigms and Organisational Analysis*. Aldershot: Ashgate.

Butterfield, K., Treviño, L. and Weaver, G. (2000) 'Moral awareness in business organizations: Influences of issue-related and social context factors', *Human Relations*, 53(7): 981–1018.

Campbell, J.P. (1990) 'The Role of Theory in Industrial and Organizational Psychology', 1: 39–74, Palo Alto, CA: Consulting Psychologists Press.

Caswell, C. and Wensley, R. (2007) 'Doors and boundaries: A recent history of the relationship between research and practice in UK organisation and management review', *Business History*, 49(2): 35–50.

Charmaz, C. (2005) 'Grounded theory in the 21st century: Applications for advancing social justice studies', in N.K. Denzin and Y.S. Lincoln (eds), *The Sage Handbook of Qualitative Research*, 3rd edn. London: Sage. pp. 507–35.

Coffey, A. (1999) *The Ethnographic Self: Fieldwork and the Representation of Reality.* London: Sage.

Colquitt, J.A. and Zapata-Phelan, C.P. (2007) 'Trends in theory building and theory testing: A five decade study of the academy of management Journal', *Academy of Management Journal*, 50(6): 1281–303.

Contu, A. and Willmott, H. (2005) 'You spin me round: The realist turn in organization and management studies', *Journal of Management Studies*, 42(8): 1645–62.

Cooperrider, D.L. and Srivastva, S. (1987) 'Appreciative inquiry in organizational life', in R. Woodman and W. Pasmore (eds), *Research in Organizational Change and Development*, Vol. 1. Greenwich: JAI Press.

Cornelissen, J. (2006) 'Making sense of theory construction: Metaphor and disciplined imagination', *Organization Studies*, 27(11): 1579–97.

Cornelissen, J., Gajewska-De Mattos, H., Piekkari, R. and Welch, C. (2012) 'Writing up as a legitimacy seeking process: Alternative publishing recipes for qualitative research', in G. Symons and C. Cassell (eds), *Qualitative Organizational Research*. London: Sage. pp. 184–203.

Cunliffe, A. (2002) 'Social poetics and management inquiry: A dialogic approach', *Journal of Management Inquiry*, 11(2): 128–46.

Cunliffe, A. (2003) 'Reflexive inquiry in organizational research: Questions and possibilities', *Human Relations*, 56(8): 983–1003.

Cunliffe, A. (2010) 'Retelling tales of the field: In search of organizational ethnography 20 years on', *Organizational Research Methods*, 13(2): 224–39.

Cunliffe, A. (2011) 'Crafting qualitative research: Morgan and Smircich 30 years on', *Organizational Research Methods*, 14(4): 647–73.

Curry, P. (2006) *Ecological Ethics: An introduction.* Cambridge: Polity.

Czarniawska, B. (1998) *A Narrative Approach to Organization Studies.* Thousand Oaks, CA: Sage.

Daft, R.L. (1980) 'The evolution of organisational analysis in ASQ 1959–1979', *Administrative Science Quarterly*, 26(2): 207–24.

Dalton, M. (1959) *Men who Manage: Fusion of Feeling and Theory in Administration.* New York: Wiley.

Dane, E. (2011) 'Changing the tune of academic writing: Muting cognitive entrenchment', *Management Inquiry*, 20(3): 332–6.

Davis, M.S. (1971) 'That's interesting!' *Philosophy and Social Science*, 1(4): 309–44.

Denzin, N.K. (1989) *The Research Act: A Theoretical Introduction to Sociological Methods*. Englewood Cliffs: Prentice-Hall.

Denzin, N. and Lincoln, Y. (2005) *The Sage Handbook of Qualitative Research,* 3rd edn. London: Sage.

Denzin, N.K. and Lincoln, Y.S. (2011) *The Sage Handbook of Qualitative Research*, 4th edn. Thousand Oaks, CA: Sage.

Derrida, J. (1976) *Of Grammatology.* Baltimore, MD: Johns Hopkins University Press.

Dickson, W.J. and Roethlisberger, F.J. (1966) *Counselling in an Organization: A Sequel to the Hawthorne Researches.* Cambridge, MA: Harvard University Press.

DiMaggio, P.J. (1995) 'Comments on What Theory is *Not*', *Administrative Science Quarterly*, 40: 391–7.

Donaldson, L. (2008) 'Following the scientific method: How I became a committed functionalist and positivist', *Organization Studies*, 26(7): 1071–88.

Easterby-Smith, M., Golden-Biddle, K. and Locke, K. (2008) 'Working with pluralism: Determining quality in qualitative research', *Organizational Research Methods,* 11(3): 419–29.

Eccles, R.G. and Nohria, N. (1992) *Beyond the Hype: Rediscovering the Essence of Management.* Harvard Business School Press.

Eden, C. and Huxham, C. (1996) 'Action research for management research', *British Journal of Management*, 7(1): 75–86.

Ehrenreich, B. (2001) *Nickel and Dimed:* On (Not) Getting By in America. London: Granta.

Eisenhardt, K.M. (1989) 'Building theories from case study research', *Academy of Management Review*, 14: 532–50.

Evered, R. and Louis, M.R. (1981) 'Alternative perspectives in the organizational sciences: "Inquiry from the inside" and "inquiry from the outside"', *Academy of Management Review*, 6(3): 385–95.

Fairclough, N. (1995) *Critical Discourse Analysis: The Critical Study of Language.* London: Longman.

Farrow, N. (1969) *Progress of Management Research*. Penguin.

Ferlie, E., McGivern, G. and De Moraes, A. (2010) 'Developing a public interest school of management', *British Journal of Management,* 21: s60–70.

Feyerabend, P. (1993) *Against Method*, 3rd edn. London: Verso.

Fincham, R. and Clark, T. (2009) 'Introduction: Can we bridge the rigor-relevance gap?' *Journal of Management Studies,* 46(3): 510–15.

Ford, J. and Harding, N. (2008) 'Fear and loathing in Harrogate, or a Study of a Conference', *Organization*, 15(2): 233–50.

Foucault, M. (1977) *Discipline and Punish: The Birth of the Prison.* Harmondsworth: Penguin.

Fox, S.(1992) 'What are we? The constitution of management in management education and human resource management', 1992b, *International Studies of Management & Organization*, 22, 3: 71–93.

Gabriel, Y. (2000) *Storytelling in Organizations: Facts, Fictions and Fantasies*. Oxford: Oxford University Press.

Garfinkel, H. (1967) *Studies in Ethnomethodology*. Englewood Cliffs, NJ: Prentice-Hall.

Geertz, C. (1974) '"From the native's point of view": On the nature of anthropological understanding', *Bulletin of the American Academy of Arts and Sciences*, 28(1): 26–45.

Gergen, K. (1999) *An Invitation to Social Construction*. Thousand Oaks, CA: Sage.

Gerring, J. (1999) What Makes a Concept Good? A Critical Framework for Understanding Concept Formation in the Social Sciences, *Polity*, 31(3): 357–93.

Gibbons, M., Camille L., Helga, N., Simon, S., Peter, S. and Martin, T. (1994) *The New Production of Knowledge: The Dynamics of Science and Research in Contemporary Societies*. London: Sage.

Giddens, A. (1984) *The Constitution of Society*. Cambridge: Polity.

Glaser, B. and Strauss, A. (1967) *The Discovery of Grounded Theory: Strategies of Qualitative Research*. London: Weidenfeld and Nicholson.

Goffman, E. (1959) *The Presentation of Self in Everyday Life*. New York: Anchor Books.

Goffman, E. (1961) *Asylums*. Harmondsworth: Penguin.

Golden-Biddle, K. and Locke, K.(1993) 'Appealing work: An investigation of how ethnographic texts convince', *Organization Science*, 4: 595–616.

Golsorkhi, D., Rouleau, L., Seidl, D. and Varra, E. (eds) (2010) *Cambridge Handbook of Strategy As Practice*. Cambridge: Cambridge University Press.

Grey, C. (2001) 'Re-imagining relevance: A response to Starkey and Madan', *British Journal of Management*, 12(3): 27–32.

Grey, C. (2009) *A Very Short, Fairly Interesting and Reasonably Cheap Book About Studying Organizations*, 2nd edn. London: Sage.

Grey, C. (2010) 'Organizing studies: Publications, politics and polemic', *Organization Studies*, 31(6): 677–94.

Grey, C. and Sinclair, A. (2006) 'Writing differently', *Organization*, 13(3): 443–53.

Guest, D. (1992) 'Right enough to be dangerously wrong', in G. Salaman (ed.), *Human Resource Strategies*. Buckingham: Open University Press. pp. 5–19.

Gummesson, E. (2000) *Qualitative Methods in Management Research*. London: Sage.

Hambrick, D. (1994) 'What if the academy actually mattered', *Academy of Management Review*, 19(1): 11–16.

Hammersley, H. (2001) 'Which side was Becker on? Questioning political and epistemological radicalism', *Qualitative Research*, 1(1): 91–110.

Handy, C. (1994) *The Empty Raincoat*. London: Arrow. p. 219.

Haney, C., Banks, C. and Zimbardo, P. (1973) 'Interpersonal dynamics in a simulated prison', *International Journal of Criminology and Penology*, 1: 69–97.

Harburg, E. (1966) 'Research map', *American Scientist*, 54: 470.

Hardy, C. (2001) 'Researching organizational discourse', *International Studies of Management and Organization*, 31(3): 25–47.

Harvey, J., Pettigrew, A. and Ferlie, E. (2002) 'The determinants of research group performance: Towards mode 2?', *Journal of Management Studies*, 39(6): 747–74.

Hassard, J. (1991) 'Multiple paradigms and organizational analysis: A case study', *Organization Studies*, 12(2): 275–99.

Hatch, M.J. (1996) 'The role of the researcher: An analysis of narrative position in organisation theory', *Journal of Management Inquiry*, 5(4): 359–74.

Herrmann, D. and Felfe, J. (2012) 'Effects of leadership style, creativity technique and personal initiative on employee creativity', *British Journal of Management*, DOI: 10.1111/j.1467-8551.2012.00849.x.

Hibbert, P., Coupland, C. and MacIntosh, R. (2010) 'Reflexivity: Recursion and relationality in organizational research processes', *Qualitative Research in Organizations and Management*, 5(1): 47–62.

Hillman, A.J. (2005) 'Reflections on service orientations, community and professions', *Academy of Management Journal*, 48(2): 185–8.

Holland, R. (1999) 'Reflexivity', *Human Relations*, 52(4): 463–84.

Homans, G. (1964) 'Contemporary theory in sociology', in R. Faris (ed.), *Handbook of Modern Sociology*. Chicago: Rand McNally. pp. 951–77.

Huczynski, A.A. (1993) 'Explaining the succession of management fads', *International Journal of Human Resource Management*, 4(2): 444–63.

Huff, A. (1999) *Writing for Scholarly Publication*. London: Sage.

Huff, A. (2000) '1999 Presidential Address: Changes in organizational knowledge production', *Academy of Management Review*, 25(2): 288–93.

Humphries, M. (2005) 'Getting personal: Reflexivity and autoethnographic vignettes', *Qualitative Inquiry*, 11(6): 840–60.

Jackson, N. and Carter, P. (1991) 'In defence of paradigm incommensurability', *Organization Studies*, 12(1): 109–27.

Johnson, P. and Duberley, J. (2000) *Understanding Management Research: An Introduction to Epistemology*. London: Sage.

Johnson, P. and Duberley, J. (2003) 'Reflexivity in management research', *Journal of Management Studies*, 40(5): 1279–303.

Jones, O. (1995) 'No guru, no method, no teacher: A critical view of (my) managerial research', *Management Learning*, 26(1): 109–27.

Kelle, U. (1997) 'Theory building in qualitative research and computer programs for the management of textual data', *Sociological Research Online*, 2(2): 1–15.

Kenny, K. (2008) 'Aesthetics and emotion in an organisational ethnography', *International Journal of Work, Organization and Emotion*, 2(4): 374–88.

Kondo, D.K. (1990) *Crafting Selves: Power, Gender and Discourses of Identity in a Japanese Workplace*. Chicago: Chicago University Press.

Kuhn, T. (1970) *The Structure of Scientific Revolutions*, 2nd edn. Chicago: University of Chicago Press.

Kunda, G. (1992) *Engineering Culture: Control and Commitment in a High-Tech Corporation*. Philadelphia: Temple University Press.

Ladyman, J. (2009) 'Impact is Created in Immeasurable Ways', *Times Higher Educational Supplement*, 12th November.

Latour, B. (1987) *Science in Action: How to Follow Scientists and Engineers through Society*. Cambridge, MA: Harvard University Press.

Lave, J. and Wenger, E. (1991) *Situated Learning: Legitimate Peripheral Participation*. Cambridge: Cambridge University Press.

Law, J. (1994) *Organizing Modernity*. Oxford: Blackwell.

Law, J. (2004) *After Method: Mess in Social Science Research*. London: Routledge.

Layder, D. (1993) *New Strategies in Social Research*. Cambridge: Polity Press.

Learmonth, M. and Humphreys, M. (2011) 'Autoethnography and academic identity: Glimpsing business school doppelgängers', *Organization*, 19(1): 99–117.

Lewin, K. (1951) *Field Theory in Social Science; Selected Theoretical Papers*, D. Cartwright, ed. New York: Harper & Row.

Lilley, S., Harvie, D., Lightfoot, G. and Weir, K. (2012) 'What are we to do with feral publishers?', *Organization*, 19(6): 905–14.

Lincoln, Y.S. and Guba, E.G. (1985) *Naturalistic Inquiry*. Thousand Oaks, CA: Sage.

Llewellyn, N. and Hindmarsh, J. (2010) *Organisation, Interaction and Practice: Studies of Real Time Work and Organising*. Cambridge: Cambridge University Press.

Locke, K. (2001) *Grounded Theory in Management Research*, London: Sage.

Locke, K. (2011) 'Field research practice in management and organisation studies: Reclaiming its traditions of discovery', *Academy of Management Annals,* 5(1): 613–52.

Locke, K., Golden-Biddle, K. and Feldman, M. (2008) 'Making doubt generative: Rethinking the role of doubt in the research process', *Organisation Studies,* 19(6): 907–18.

Lofland, J. and Lofland, L.H. (1995) *Analysing Social Settings: A Guide to Qualitative Observation and Analysis.* Belmont, CA: Wadsworth.

Lupton, T. (1963) *On the Shop Floor: Two Studies of Workshop Organization and Output.* London: Pergamon.

Lupton, T. (1985) *Let the Data Speak!* Manchester Business School, MBS Working Paper Series.

Macdonald, S. and Kam, J. (2007) 'Ring a Ring o' Roses: Quality journals and gamesmanship in management studies', *Journal of Management Studies,* 44(4): 640–55.

MacIntyre, A. (1971) 'A perspective on philosophy', *Social Research: An International Quarterly Critical Perspectives on the Social Sciences,* 38 (3).

March, J. (2000) 'Plenary Address, European Group for Organization Studies Conference', Helsinki, Finland, July.

Marshall, J. (1995) *Women Managers Moving On: Exploring Career and Life Choices.* London: Routledge.

Meho, L.I. (2007) 'The rise and rise of citation analysis', *Physics World,* January, 32–6.

Merton, R. (1940) 'Bureaucratic Structure and Personality', *Social Forces,* May: 560–8.

Miles, M.B. (1979) 'Qualitative data as an attractive nuisance: The problem of analysis', *Administrative Science Quarterly,* 24: 590–601.

Miles, M.B. and Huberman, A.M. (1994) *Qualitative Data Analysis: An Expanded Sourcebook,* 2nd edn. Thousand Oaks, CA: Sage.

Mintzberg, H. (1973) *The Nature of Managerial Work.* New York: Harper & Row.

Morgan, G. (ed.) (1983) *Beyond Method: Strategies for Social Research.* London: Sage.

Morgan, G. and Smircich, L. (1980) 'The case for qualitative research', *Academy of Management Review,* 5(4): 491–500.

Neyland, D. (2008) *Organizational Ethnography.* London: Sage.

Northcraft, G.B. and Tenbrunsel, A.E. (2012) 'Publications, contributions and the social dilemma of scholarly productivity: A reaction to Aguinis, Debruin, Cunningham, Hall, Culpepper and Gottfredson', *Academy of Management Learning and Education,* 11(2): 303–8.

Orr, J. (1996) *Talking About Machines: An Ethnography of a Modern Job.* Ithaca: Cornell University Press.

Owen, D. and Strong, T.B. (2004) 'Introduction' in M. Weber, *The Vocation Lectures: 'Science as a Vocation, Politics as a Vocation'*. Indianapolis: Hackett Publishing.

Parry, K. and Boyle, M. (2009) 'Organizational autoethnography', in D. Buchanan and A. Bryman (eds), *The Sage Handbook of Organizational Research Methods*. London: Sage.

Perrow, C. (1995) 'Journaling careers', in L.L. Cummings and P.J. Frost (eds), *Publishing in the Organizational Sciences*. Thousand Oaks, CA: Sage.

Peters, T. and Waterman, R. (1982) *In Search of Excellence*. New York: Harper & Row.

Pettigrew, A.M. (2001) 'Management research after modernisation', *British Journal of Management*, 12: S61–S76.

Pfeffer, J. (1993) 'Barriers to the advance of organizational science: Paradigm development as a dependent variable', *Academy of Management Review*, 18(4): 599–620.

Phillips E.M. And Pugh, D.S. (2005) *How To Get a PhD: A Handbook for Students and Their Supervisors,* 4th edn, Maidenhead: Open University Press.

Potter, J. and Wetherell, M. (1987) *Discourse and Social Psychology: Beyond Attitudes and Behaviour.* London: Sage.

Prasad, A. (2005) *Crafting Qualitative Research: Working in the Postpositivist Traditions*. Armonk, NY: M.E. Sharpe.

Prasad, A. and Prasad, P. (2002) 'The coming of age of interpretive organisational research', *Organizational Research Methods,* 5: 4–11.

Pratt, M.G. (2009) 'For the lack of a boilerplate: Tips on writing up and reviewing qualitative research', *Academy of Management Journal,* 52(5): 856–62.

Pugh, D. (1981) 'The Aston program perspective', in A.H. Van de Ven and W.F. Joyce (eds), *Perspectives on Organization Design and Behavior.* Wiley-Interscience. pp.135–66.

Reed, M. (1992) 'Introduction', in Reed, M. and Hughes, M. *Rethinking Organization: On New Directions in Organization Theory and Analysis,* London: Sage.

Reed, M. (2005) 'Reflections on the "realist turn" in organization and management studies', *Journal of Management Studies,* 42(8): 1621–44.

Revans, R.W. (1982) *The Origins and Growth of Action Learning.* Bromley: Chartwell Bratt.

Riach, K. (2009) 'Exploring participant-centred reflexivity in the research interview', *Sociology,* 43(2): 356–70.

Richards, T. and Richards, L. (1998) 'Using computers in qualitative research', in N.K. Denzin and Y. Lincoln (eds), *Collecting and Interpreting Qualitative Materials*. London: Sage.

Roethlisberger, F.J. and Dickson, W.J. (1939) *Management and the Worker: An Account of a Research Programme Conducted by the Western Electric Company, Hawthorne Works, Chicago*. Cambridge, MA: Harvard University Press.

Rorty, R. (1979) *Philosophy and the Mirror of Nature*. Princeton, New Jersey: Princeton University Press.

Rousseau, D.M. (2006) 'Is there such a thing as evidence-based management?' *Academy of Management Review*, 31(2): 256–69.

Rowlinson, M., Booth, C., Clark, P., Delahaye, A. and Procter, S. (2010) 'Social remembering and organizational memory', *Organization Studies*, 31(1): 69–87.

Roy, D. (1958) 'Banana time: Job satisfaction and informal interaction', *Human Organization*, 18: 156–68.

Rynes, S.L. (2005) 'Taking Stock and Looking Ahead', *Academy of Management Journal*, 48: 732–7.

Saldaña, J. (2008) 'Popular film as an instructional strategy in qualitative research methods courses', *Qualitative Inquiry*, 15(1): 247–61.

Sandberg, J. (2005) 'How do we justify knowledge produced within interpretive approaches?', *Organizational Research Methods*, 8: 41–68.

Sandberg, J. and Alvesson, M. (2011) 'Ways of constructing research questions: Gap spotting or problematization?', *Organization*, 18(1): 23–44.

Saussure, F. de (1916) *Course in General Linguistics*. London: Fontana/Collins.

Sayer, A. (1984) *Method in Social Science: A Realist Approach* (2nd edition 1992). London: Routledge.

Schon, D. (1983) *The Reflective Practitioner: How Professionals Think in Action*. London: Maurice Temple Smith.

Schwandt, T.A. (1997) *Qualitative Inquiry: A Dictionary of Terms*, London: Sage.

Schwartzman, H.B. (1993) *Ethnography in Organizations*, Qualitative Research Methods Series 27. Newbury Park, CA: Sage.

Shrivastava, P. (1987) 'Rigor and practical usefulness of research in strategic management', *Strategic Management Journal*, 8(1): 77–92.

Simmel, G. (1950) 'The stranger', in K.H. Wolff (ed.), *The Sociology of Georg Simmel*. New York: The Free Press.

Spicer, A. (2005) 'Conferences', in C. Jones and D. O'Doherty (eds), *Manifestos for the Business School of Tomorrow*. Abo: Dvalin Books. pp. 21–7.

Spradley, J.P. and McCurdy, D.W. (1972) *The Cultural Experience: Ethnography in Complex Society*. Chicago: Science Research Associates.

Starbuck, W.H. (1981) 'A trip to view the elephants and rattlesnakes in the garden of Aston', in A.H. Van de Ven and W.F. Joyce (eds), *Perspectives on Organization Design and Behavior*. Wiley-Interscience. pp. 167–98.

Starbuck, W.H. (2005) 'How much better are the most-prestigious journals? The statistics of academic publication', *Organization Science*, 16(2): 180–200.

Sutton, R. I. and Staw, B.M. (1995) 'What theory is *not*', *Administrative Science Quarterly,* 40(3): 371–384.

Terkel, S. (1977) *Working: People Talk About What They Do All Day and How They Feel About What They Do*. Harmondsworth: Penguin.

Thomas, H. and Wilson, D. (2011) '"Physics envy", cognitive legitimacy or practical relevance: Dilemmas in the evolution of management research in the UK', *British Journal of Management,* 19 August. DOI: 10.1111/j.1467-8551.2011.00766.x.

Thorpe, R. and Beasley, A. (2006) 'The characteristics of performance management research: Implications and challenges, *International Journal of Productivity and Performance Management*, 53(4): 334–44.

Thorpe, R. and Holt, R. (2008) *The SAGE Dictionary of Qualitative Management Research*. London: Sage.

Tranfield, D. and Starkey, K. (1998), 'The nature, social organisation and promotion of management research: Towards policy', *British Journal of Management*, 9: 341–53.

Troeltsch, E. (1912) *The Social Teachings of the Christian Churches*. London: Allen and Unwin.

Van de Ven, A. (1989) 'Nothing so practical as a good theory', *Academy of Management Review,* 14: 486–9.

Van de Ven, A. (2007) *Engaged Scholarship: A Guide for Organizational and Social Research*. Oxford: Oxford University Press.

Van de Ven, A. and Poole, M.S. (1995) 'Explaining development and change in organizations', *The Academy of Management Review,* 20(3): 510–40.

Van Maanen, J. (1988) *Tales of the Field: On Writing Ethnography*. Chicago: University of Chicago Press.

Van Maanen, J. (1995) 'Style as theory', *Organization Science,* 6(1): 133–43.

Van Maanen, J. and Kolb, D. (1985) 'The professional apprentice: Observations of fieldwork roles in two organisational settings', *Research in the Sociology of Organizations*, 4: 1–33.

Vogel, R. (2012) 'The visible colleges of management and organization studies: A bibliometric analysis of academic journals', *Organization Studies*, 33(8): 1015–43.

Watson, T. (1994) *In Search of Management: Culture, Chaos and Control in Managerial Work*. London: Routledge.

Watson, T. (1996) 'Motivation: That's Maslow, isn't it?', *Management Learning*, 27(4): 447–64.

Weber, M. (2009) 'Science as a vocation', in H.H. Gerth and C. Wright Mills (eds), *From Max Weber: Essays in Sociology*. London: Routledge.

Weick, K. (1969) *The Social Psychology of Organising*. New York: McGraw Hill.

Weick, K.E. (1989) 'Theory Construction as Disciplined Imagination', *Academy of Management Review*, 14(4): 516–31.

Weick, K.E. (1995) 'What theory is *not*, theorizing *is*', *Administrative Science Quarterly*, 40: 385–90.

Weick, K. (2001) 'Gapping the relevance bridge: Fashions meet fundamentals in management research', *British Journal of Management*, 12(3): 71–5.

Weick, K.E. (2002) 'Real time reflexivity: Prods to reflection', *Organization Studies*, 23(6): 893–8.

Wenger, E. (2000) 'Communities of practice and social learning systems', *Organization*, 7(2): 225–46.

Whetten, D.A. (1989) 'What constitutes a theoretical contribution?, *Academy of Management Journal*, 43: 1265–82.

Whitehead, A.N. (1929) *Process and Reality: An Essay in Cosmology*. New York: Free Press.

Whitley, R. (1984) *The Intellectual and Social Organization of the Sciences*. Oxford: Clarendon Press.

Whittington, R. (2006) 'Completing the practice turn in strategy research', *Organization Studies*, 27(5): 613–34.

Willmott, H. (1990) 'Beyond paradigmatic closure in organisational enquiry', in J. Hassard and D. Pym (eds), *The Theory and Philosophy of Organizations*. London: Routledge. pp. 44–60.

Willmott, H. (2011) 'Journal list fetishism and the perversion of scholarship: Reactivity and the ABS list', *Organization*, 18(4): 429–42.

Wilson, J.F. (1992) *Manchester Experiment: The History of Manchester Business School (1965–1990)*. London: Paul Chapman Publishing.

Wolcott, H.F. (1999) *Ethnography: A Way of Seeing*. Walnut Creek: Alta Mira.

Wray-Bliss, E. (2003) 'Research subjects/research subjections: Exploring the ethics and politics of critical research', *Organization*, 10(2): 307–25.

Wright Mills, C. (1959) *The Sociological Imagination*. New York: Oxford University Press.

Yanow, D. (2003) 'Interpretive empirical political science: What makes this not a subfield of qualitative methods', *Qualitative Methods: Newsletter of the American Political Science Association Organised Section on Qualitative Methods*, 1(2): 9–13.

Yanow, D. and Schwartz-Shea, P. (eds) (2006) *Interpretation and Method: Empirical Research Methods and the Interpretive Turn*. Armonk, NY: M.E. Sharpe.

Ybema, S., Yanow, D., Wels, H. and Kamsteeg, F. (2009) *Organizational Ethnography: Studying the Complexities of Everyday Life*. London: Sage.

Yin, R. (1984) *Case Study Research*. Beverley Hills, CA: Sage.

Zbaracki, M.J. (1998) 'The rhetoric and reality of total quality management', *Administrative Science Quarterly*, 43: 602–36.

Zerubavel, E. (1981) *Hidden Rhythms: Schedules and Calendars in Social Life*. Chicago: University of Chicago Press.

Zickar, M.J. and Carter, N.T. (2010) 'Reconnecting with the spirit of workplace ethnography: A historical review', *Organizational Research Methods*, 13(2): 304–19.

Ziliak, S.T. and McCloskey, D.N. (2008) *The Cult of Statistical Significance: How the Standard Error Cost Us Jobs, Justice and Lives*. Ann Arbor: University of Michigan Press.

Index